Oxfo

Sha

OXFORD SHAKESPEARE TOPICS

Published and Forthcoming Titles Include:

Oxford Shakespeare Topics

GENERAL EDITORS: PETER HOLLAND AND STANLEY WELLS

Shakespeare and Women

PHYLLIS RACKIN

OXFORD
UNIVERSITY PRESS

OXFORD

UNIVERSITY PRESS

Great Clarendon Street, Oxford OX2 6DP

Oxford University Press is a department of the University of Oxford.
It furthers the University's objective of excellence in research, scholarship,
and education by publishing worldwide in

Oxford New York

Auckland Cape Town Dar es Salaam Hong Kong Karachi
Kuala Lumpur Madrid Melbourne Mexico City Nairobi
New Delhi Shanghai Taipei Toronto
With offices in

Argentina Austria Brazil Chile Czech Republic France Greece
Guatemala Hungary Italy Japan South Korea Poland Portugal
Singapore Switzerland Thailand Turkey Ukraine Vietnam

Oxford is a registered trade mark of Oxford University Press
in the UK and in certain other countries

Published in the United States
by Oxford University Press Inc., New York

ISBN 978-0-19-818694-6

Printed in the United Kingdom by
Lightning Source UK Ltd., Milton Keynes

for Donald Rackin

Acknowledgements

I am indebted to many good teachers and magnanimous friends for helpful readings, stimulating questions, good advice, and sympathetic encouragement. Among them, I especially want to thank Rebecca Bushnell, Grace Ioppolo, Ann Rosalind Jones, Lena Cowen Orlin, Peter Stallybrass, the Medieval/Renaissance group at the University of Pennsylvania, and Stanley Wells and Peter Holland, the editors of 'Oxford Shakespeare Topics'. I am also grateful for the generous and efficient assistance of Andrew McNeillie and Tom Perridge at Oxford University Press; John Pollack, Michael Ryan, and Daniel Traister at the Rare Book and Manuscript Library at the University of Pennsylvania; and Georgianna Ziegler at the Folger Shakespeare Library. Most of all, I am indebted to Donald Rackin and Jean E. Howard. They read everything, and the entire project from beginning to end was energized by their intellectual challenge and sustained by their emotional support.

An earlier version of Chapter 1 was published under the title 'Misogyny is Everywhere' in Dympna Callaghan (ed.), *A Feminist Companion to Shakespeare* (Oxford: Blackwell, 2000), pp. 42–58. Chapter 4 incorporates material from my essays 'Shakespeare's Cross-dressing Comedies' in *A Companion to Shakespeare's Works Volume III: The Comedies*, edited by Richard Dutton and Jean E. Howard (Oxford: Blackwell, 2003), pp. 114–36; and 'Shakespeare's Boy Cleopatra, the Decorum of Nature, and the Golden World of Poetry', *PMLA* 87 (March, 1972), pp. 201–12. Chapter 6 incorporates material from my essay 'Dating Shakespeare's Women', *Shakespeare Jahrbuch* 134 (1998), pp. 29–43.

Contents

List of Illustrations

Introduction

This book situates Shakespeare's representations of women in a variety of historical contexts ranging from the early modern English world in which they were first conceived to the contemporary Western world in which our own encounters with them are staged. In so doing, it also challenges some of the assumptions that currently shape our efforts to understand Shakespeare's representations of women historically.

The last thirty years have witnessed an impressive and very influential body of scholarly work on this subject, but I believe it is time to reconsider the stories that that work has produced. When I use the word 'stories' here, I do not mean it in a pejorative sense to imply that the work produced by recent feminist/historicist scholarship is merely fictional or that it can be replaced by a factual history that could somehow avoid the telling of stories. As Hayden White argued over twenty-five years ago, all history writing is a form of story-telling because it necessarily requires the selection and arrangement of evidence to construct a meaningful narrative. As White explained,

> no set of casually recorded historical events can in itself constitute a story: the most it might offer to the historian are story *elements*. The events are *made* into a story by the suppression or subordination of certain of them and the highlighting of others, by characterization, motific repetition, variation of tone and point of view, alternative descriptive strategies, and the like—in short, all of the techniques that we would normally expect to find in the emplotment of a novel or a play.[1]

One of the effects that White attributes to this process of emplotment is particularly relevant to our attempts to construct a historical context for Shakespeare's women. Once the story has been constructed, he proposed, whatever historical data it incorporates will become familiarized:

> The original strangeness, mystery, or exoticism of the events is dispelled, and they take on a familiar aspect, not in their details, but in their functions as a familiar kind of configuration. They are familiarized, not only because the

reader now has more *information* about the events, but also because he has been shown how the data conform to an *icon* of a comprehensible finished process, a plot structure with which he is familiar as part of his cultural endowment. (p. 86)

White made this argument at a time when the masculine pronoun 'he' was still the preferred form for designating 'the reader', implying either that most readers were likely to be men or that the gender of the reader was irrelevant. In my own appropriation of White's argument, I am assuming that the gender of the reader is indeed relevant, as is her or his commitment to the feminist political project. For readers who share that commitment, I think we have reached a point where we need to engage in a kind of iconoclasm in regard to the familiar plot structures that have configured many of the stories we have been telling both about women's roles in Shakespeare's plays and about the roles women were assigned in Shakespeare's England. As I argue in Chapter 1, these stories have too often emphasized patriarchal power, male misogyny, and women's oppression. No one can deny that there is ample evidence to support the grim stories we have been telling. But although we cannot afford to ignore the history of women's subjugation, we cannot afford to rest in it either. Overestimating past repression can easily slip into a dangerous complacency about present progress.

The familiar stories of women's oppression in Shakespeare's world have proved difficult to displace even as recent historical scholarship has provided the material for alternative narratives. In Chapter 2 I review some of this material. We now know, for instance, that a great many women exercised their own choice in negotiating marriages for themselves and for other women as well, but we still tend to assume that patriarchal control was the norm. We also know that the majority of executors of wills in Shakespeare's England were women, but we still assume that most women were deprived of economic power and authority. We now have evidence of women's widespread participation in pre-Reformation drama, but we still tend to assume that women's exclusion from the London professional companies followed a long-standing tradition of all-male performance. We know that in Shakespeare's London, women were a visible presence all over the city, including the playhouses, but we still tend to assume that Shakespeare's plays should be read from the point of view of a male spectator who would have responded to representations of women's power and autonomy as occasions for anxious hostility.

Given the difficulty of rethinking our basic assumptions about women's places in Shakespeare's world, it is tempting to abandon the work of trying to see their roles in his plays in historical context. Turning to a contemplation of the texts themselves to articulate the meanings they have for us in the here and now of our own imaginative experience might look like a better alternative, but even if we do so, history will impose its formidable force. The current prestige of history in academic Shakespeare scholarship makes it a ground that feminists can ill afford to forfeit. Moreover, whether or not we acknowledge their presence, both the historical legacy we inherit and the historical location we inhabit will shape and limit our responses to the plays. Which plays will we choose to study? Which plays will be chosen for us by theatrical producers, scholarly editors, the organizers of academic conferences, and the shapers of school curricula? Will we read or see *The Taming of the Shrew* or *The Merry Wives of Windsor*? *Hamlet* or *Antony and Cleopatra*? *Henry V* or *King John*? The pressures of our own historical location in determining those choices are the subject of Chapter 3, 'Our Canon, Ourselves', where I argue that the plays— and the aspects of those plays—that we have chosen to emphasize tell us more about our own assumptions regarding women than about the beliefs that informed the responses of Shakespeare's first audiences. In particular, I focus on two plays that offer a striking illustration of the current preference for performances of women's oppression: *The Taming of the Shrew*, which has enjoyed remarkable popularity in recent years, and *The Merry Wives of Windsor*, which has been much less frequently performed or discussed. Even the titles suggest some of the differences between the two plays. One promises a misogynist fable about a generic 'shrew' who is tamed, while the other offers a cheerful portrait of merry wives who live in a specific English town.

This awareness of the ways our own interests, desires, and anxieties shape our encounters with the past is a crucial form of historical knowledge, as is the recognition that our own encounters with Shakespeare's plays are inevitably different from those of his original audiences. In the case of his female characters, the most striking and best-known manifestation of that difference is the fact that all of his women's roles were originally designed to be performed by male actors. This practice has received considerable attention in recent scholarship, but there is very little consensus in regard to what it tells us about early modern understandings of sex and gender. The implications of cross-dressed performance in a playhouse where it was customary and in a culture in which the modern, Western sex/gender system was not yet in place would have been significantly different from its implications in a modern, Western theatre, but the extent and nature of those differences are still subjects of intense debate. What happened when female characters whose roles were performed by male actors in female costumes adopted male disguise? What kind of erotic excitement was generated by the spectacle of a love scene when both of the actors who performed it were male and both were dressed in male costumes? Did transvestite performance destabilize or reinforce the gender norms of the represented action? Did the absence of women from Shakespeare's stage mean that the plays expressed an exclusively masculine point of view? Chapter 4 brings a feminist/historicist perspective to these questions in order to explain why, although femininity on Shakespeare's stage was always a show to be performed, the absence of female performers does not invalidate the enthusiastic responses his female characters have always elicited from women or foreclose their possibilities as models for feminist appropriation.

Of all Shakespeare's work, the texts that seem most resistant to feminist appropriation are the sonnets. Because the sonnets were written in the first person, they come to us not as the utterances of characters in a dramatic fiction but as expressions of the speaker's own feelings and beliefs. When a woman is described, her representation is not mediated by the presence of a male actor performing her part. This appearance of unmediated self-expression makes it tempting to read the sonnets as a record of Shakespeare's own personal feelings, but the feelings they express are often deeply—even pathologically— misogynistic. The speaker has at least two loves, a fair young man whom he describes as his 'better angel' and a dark woman whom he calls his 'worser spirit' (Sonnet 144).[2] In contrast to the beautiful, aristocratic young man, the woman is physically 'foul' (Sonnet 137), sexually promiscuous, and morally despicable. Some of these so-called 'dark lady' sonnets express a furious loathing for the woman's body and for heterosexual passion itself, which the speaker denounces as the 'expense of spirit in a waste of shame' (Sonnet 129).

We will probably never know to what extent Shakespeare's sonnets contain autobiographical revelations. What we do know is that he wrote them towards the end of a long tradition of sonneteering, which had already established the conventions that defined both the writer's task and his original readers' expectations. Chapter 5 situates Shakespeare's sonnets within that tradition, which, as recent feminist critics have demonstrated, was itself inherently misogynistic. Although the traditional sonnets were ostensibly designed to express the writer's devotion to a beautiful, unattainable lady, their true subject was always the writer himself, and their true purpose was to display the writer's virtuosity in competition with other sonneteers. The lady is typically objectified as an aggregate of impossibly idealized features, which dehumanize her and constitute an implicit rejection of the imperfect bodies of actual women. Shakespeare's rewriting of the idealized Petrarchan lady, whether or not it contains autobiographical revelations, brilliantly anticipates this critical analysis. In his sonnets, as in his plays, the power and eloquence of his writing and the cultural authority it carries make his work important to women readers, not because it tells us what Shakespeare thought and felt about women but because of what it enables us to think and feel about ourselves.

The final chapter focuses on an issue that is implicit in all the others—the place of Shakespeare's women in history. For over four hundred years, the roles of Shakespeare's female characters have been repeatedly updated to make them comprehensible in terms of new conceptions of women's nature and women's roles in the world. The history of these changes can be studied both in the records of theatrical productions and in readers' comments about the plays, and they offer considerable insight into the roles that actual women have been expected to play in the disparate worlds in which the plays have been performed and read. Paradoxically, however, this implication of Shakespeare's female characters in the process of historical change has tended to occlude their own historicity, as they served, and continue to serve, in ever-changing guises as models of an unchanging, universal female nature.

Our own experience of Shakespeare's women is conditioned not only by the accumulated tradition of Shakespeare scholarship and reception but also by the present history of the world in which we live: both of these histories help to shape our experience of the plays, whether we study them in an academic setting, see them on stage or screen, or read them in the privacy of our own rooms. Both of these histories will need feminist intervention in the twenty-first century.

1

A Usable History

In 1999, *The New York Times Magazine* devoted a series of special issues to topics relating to the coming millennium. The topic on 16 May was women's history, and although many subjects were addressed and many writers participated (some of them well-known authorities), most of the articles were remarkably consistent in contrasting the dismal past with the present achievements of women in such diverse fields as medicine, government, economics, religion, law, and education. As such, they expressed the dominant view of women's history in our time. I am sure the *Times* got its facts right, but other facts might have been chosen to construct an entirely different story. To choose only the most obvious example, although women in the Western democracies now have the right to vote, the highest elective offices in those countries are generally reserved for men. In Shakespeare's time, by contrast, England and Scotland were both ruled by female monarchs, and Catherine de' Medici was the regent of France.

Neither story is complete. Shakespeare lived in a time and place when women were excluded from the universities and the learned professions, married women lost the right to their own property unless special provisions were made to preserve it, and wife-beating was regarded as a perfectly acceptable means of resolving domestic disputes. In that same time and place, however, aristocratic women managed great estates and wielded economic power comparable to that of the head of a large modern corporation; and women lower on the social scale were active in trades that are now regarded as 'traditionally male'. The construction of a historical narrative inevitably involves multiple selections. The records that supply the materials for that narrative are themselves the product of a long process of record-keeping, which is conditioned at every point by the personal motivations and institutional constraints that determined what information would be recorded and which records would be kept and retrieved. And the final stage, the selection of the materials for an historical narrative, is similarly constrained by the resources and limitations, both personal and professional, of the historian who makes the selection.

The historical narratives we choose (or have chosen for us) have consequences for the present and future, and if the story of misogyny and oppression is the only story we tell about the past, we risk a dangerous complacency in the present. Like the advertisements for Virginia Slims cigarettes that repeatedly told American women 'You've come a long way, baby' because they could now smoke openly rather than hiding their habits from their menfolk, an oversimplified history that emphasizes past oppression is likely to encourage an equally oversimplified optimism about the present situation. As Lena Cowen Orlin observes, 'if we have enjoyed this construction of women, perhaps it is because it offers us the comforting reassurance that history has made progress and that we have come a long way (baby) from our early modern predecessors':

Literary historians have so often repeated the mantra that women were enjoined . . . to be chaste, silent, and obedient; have so often described the spatial restrictions on women; and have so often 'explained' playtexts in terms taken from the most conservative literatures of their time that the reigning orthodoxy of historiography has become that of patriarchal ideology. I and perhaps others have been seduced by the mere effort of research into thinking these prescriptions were culturally operative in a way that they cannot have been in many women's daily lives. Even though we have told ourselves that such admonitions would not have been necessary had their strictures been generally observed, we have nonetheless persisted in depicting women as victims of unrelenting misogyny, patriarchy, and oppression. It may be that we have been writing the history that our culture seems to have required of us.[1]

Versions of that history have dominated both popular and scholarly thinking about the world in which Shakespeare wrote. They can be found virtually everywhere there is a discussion of women's place in Shakespeare's England, from introductory classrooms to the pages of the most learned scholarly publications. Here is one of many possible examples, taken from the pages of *Shakespeare Quarterly*:

Misogyny presents an interpretive embarrassment of riches: it is everywhere, unabashed in its articulation and so overdetermined in its cultural roots that individual instances sometimes seem emotionally underdetermined, rote and uninflected expressions of what would go without saying if it weren't said so often.[2]

'In historical research', as a wise old teacher once warned me, 'you're likely to find what you are looking for'; and what most of us have been looking for in recent years is a history of men's anxiety in the face of female power, of women's disempowerment, and of outright misogyny. We need to interrogate that history (and, as Orlin suggests, our reasons for preferring it), not because it is necessarily incorrect but because it is incomplete. It constitutes only one of many stories that could be told about women's place in Shakespeare's world, and I think we need to consider the implications of its current hegemony. Why does the evidence for misogyny in Shakespeare's world strike the writer as 'an embarrassment of riches'? Who is enriched by the many 'rote and uninflected expressions of what would go without saying if it weren't said so often' in recent feminist criticism?

One reason the story of patriarchal oppression has become so influential is that it has been disseminated in classrooms and textbooks. The editor of a recent reader designed to illustrate *The Cultural Identity of Seventeenth-Century Woman*, for instance, states flatly that

Woman's place was within doors, her business domestic. . . . Women of evident intelligence themselves accepted this divorce between the private (feminine) and public (masculine) spheres and, despite the recent precedents of Mary Queen of Scots, Mary Tudor and Elizabeth, they shared the age's 'distaste . . . for the notion of women's involvement in politics.'[3]

Even the most sophisticated scholarship often includes similar claims. For example, in what is likely to become a standard history of gender in early modern England, Anthony Fletcher writes,

It was conventional, as we have seen, to assume men and women had clearly defined gender roles indoors and out of doors. . . . Femininity, as we have seen, was presented as no more than a set of negatives. The requirement of chastity was, as we have seen, the overriding measure of female gender. Woman not only had to be chaste but had to be seen to be chaste: silence, humility and modesty were the signifiers that she was so.[4]

Some of the most important recent feminist/historicist literary scholarship includes reminders that 'the period was fraught with anxiety about rebellious women and particularly their rebellion through language';[5] that 'women's reading was policed and their writing prohibited or marked as transgressive even when they were not engaged in other criminal activities';[6] and that 'an obsessive energy was invested in exerting control over the unruly woman—the woman who was exercising either her sexuality or her tongue under her own control rather than under the rule of a man'.[7] In a sense, of course, these quotations are misleading because they are taken out of context, and they belie the subtlety and complexity of the arguments from which they were taken. Nonetheless, I believe the excerpts are significant because they indicate how often even the best feminist scholarship feels the need to situate itself within a patriarchal master narrative.

Feminist scholars found a brilliant explication of that narrative in Peter Stallybrass's essay, 'Patriarchal Territories: The Body Enclosed', which argued that women's bodies were assumed to be '*naturally* "grotesque" ' and that women were therefore 'subjected to constant surveillance . . . because, as Bakhtin says of the grotesque body, it is "unfinished, outgrows itself, transgresses its own limits" '. This constant surveillance, Stallybrass continued, focused on 'three specific areas: the mouth, chastity, the threshold of the house', which 'were frequently collapsed into each other', 'Silence, the closed mouth, is made a sign of chastity. And silence and chastity are, in turn, homologous to woman's enclosure within the house.'[8] Published in 1986, 'Patriarchal Territories' theorized the relationships between sexual loathing, the silencing of women's voices, and the constriction of women's activities in a beautifully articulated analysis that proved to have remarkable influence and explanatory power in subsequent feminist criticism. It is significant, I believe, that the conclusion of Stallybrass's article, where he suggested that the figure of the unruly woman was also valorized during the period as a rallying point for protest against social injustice, was much less influential and, in fact, usually ignored.

The pervasive scholarly investment in Renaissance misogyny led to a massive rereading of Shakespeare's plays. As Valerie Traub observes,

'It is by now a commonplace that Shakespeare was preoccupied with the uncontrollability of women's sexuality; witness the many plots concerning the need to prove female chastity, the threat of adultery, and, even when female fidelity is not a major theme of the play, the many references to cuckoldry in songs, jokes, and passing remarks.'[9] Reminders that women were expected to be chaste, silent, and obedient probably occur more frequently in recent scholarship than they did in the literature of Shakespeare's time; the connections between female speech and female sexual transgression are retraced and the anxieties evoked by the possibility of female power are discovered in play after play. 'Female sexuality in Shakespeare's plays', we are told, 'is invariably articulated as linguistic transgression—that is, a verbal replication of female obliquity.'[10] If speech is transgressive, reading and writing are even more dangerous. When Lavinia in *Titus Andronicus* is displayed on stage with 'her hands cut off and her tongue cut out, and ravished' (S.D. 2.4.1), the gruesome spectacle is 'expressive of the anxieties she generates as an educated, and hence potentially unruly, woman'.[11]

Plays with overtly repressive and misogynist themes have proved increasingly popular, and the stories they tell are held up as historically accurate expressions of beliefs generally endorsed in Shakespeare's time. *The Taming of the Shrew*, for instance, is the subject of 246 listings for the years 1980–2003 in the online *MLA Bibliography*, far more than any of the other early comedies (for those same years, the *Bibliography* lists 90 for *The Two Gentlemen of Verona*, 101 for *The Comedy of Errors*, and 136 for *Love's Labour's Lost*).[12] Other plays are reinterpreted. *The Merchant of Venice*, for example, 'instructs its audience that daughters who submit, who know their place, will ultimately fare better than daughters who rebel'.[13] The heroines of Shakespeare's middle comedies were especially attractive to the feminist critics of the 1970s, when it seemed important to mobilize Shakespeare's authority in the service of women's own political goals. In the 1980s, however, a more pessimistic picture emerged as scholars marshalled historical evidence to demonstrate the pervasiveness of patriarchal beliefs and practices and to discredit the optimistic feminist readings of the 1970s as unhistorical.

Although one of the characteristics that traditionally made the heroines of Shakespeare's middle comedies attractive was their erotic appeal, influential critics now associated that attraction with the fact that they were portrayed by male actors. Stephen Greenblatt's widely cited article on 'Fiction and Friction' associated this practice with Thomas Laqueur's argument that Renaissance anatomical theory constructed a single-sexed model of the human body to argue that 'the open secret of identity—that within differentiated individuals is a single structure, identifiably male—is presented literally in the all-male cast'. Although many Renaissance writers argued that women's bodies were essentially different from men's, Laqueur emphasized the Galenic theories that homologies between the structures of male and female genital organs showed that women's genitals were simply inferior versions of men's except that they were turned inside out and located inside rather than outside the body. For Greenblatt, this belief enabled plays like *Twelfth Night* to dramatize the fact that 'men love women precisely as *representations*, a love the original performances of these plays literalized in the person of the boy actor'.[14] For Lisa Jardine, the heroines of these plays were 'sexually enticing *qua* transvestied boys, and the plays encourage the audience to view them as such'.[15] Moreover, at the same time that criticism like Greenblatt's and Jardine's taught us to recognize that cross-dressed boys may have been objects of desire for Shakespeare's original audience, we were also taught that sexualized women were not: female sexual desire, we are repeatedly told, was regarded as threatening. In *Antony and Cleopatra*, for instance, 'Egypt's queen ... resembles other Jacobean females who in desiring or being desired become a source of pollution'.[16] In *Henry VI, Part 2*, depicting 'Margaret as a figure of open and unrestrained sexual passion is one way of demonizing her and representing the dangers of a femininity not firmly under the control of a father or husband'.[17]

Sexual passion is not the only characteristic that makes women threatening in recent feminist Shakespeare criticism, where it seems that virtually any manifestation of female strength or ability, even if it is admired by other characters on stage, would have had to evoke anxiety in the original audiences. Helen in *All's Well that Ends Well* is a good example. In the playtext her virtues are celebrated and her aspirations endorsed by the King and the Countess. Anne Barton's introduction to the play in *The Riverside Shakespeare* summed up the traditional view of the character: 'Helena is prized by the older generation not only because they recognize her intrinsic worth, but because she is a living example of the attitudes of the past.'[18] She is also the centre of dramatic interest, with the longest part in the play. According to Marvin Spevack's *Concordance* to Shakespeare's works, she speaks 15.858 per cent of the words in the script; Bertram speaks only 9.042 per cent, a total that is exceeded not only by Helen, but also by Bertram's mother, who has 9.618 per cent.[19] Nonetheless, according to Peter Erickson, a leading male feminist critic,

Helena's gender makes impossible any one-sided identification with Helena against Bertram.... Reacting against Helena's triumph, Shakespeare remains in part sympathetically bound to the besieged male positions of both Bertram and the king; the play thereby gives voice not only to the two male characters' discomfiture but also to Shakespeare's. The authorial division that blocks a convincing resolution is significant because it dramatizes a much larger cultural quandary: the society's inability to accommodate, without deep disturbance, decisive female control.[20]

The last two sentences are carefully worded, attributing ambivalence about Helen's achievement and anxiety about the spectacle of 'decisive female control' to Shakespeare and to the culture in which he wrote, thus authorizing ambivalence and anxiety as the historically appropriate responses to Helen's triumph. But the first sentence I quoted— 'Helena's gender makes impossible any one-sided identification with Helena against Bertram'—seems to claim even more. The present tense of the verb seems to universalize Erickson's reading and deny its historical specificity, implying that ambivalence and anxiety are the only possible responses to the character for any reader or viewer in any time or place.

It may be unfair to make so much of Erickson's use of the present tense, but that usage points to a larger problem for historicist literary criticism, which has pressing implications for feminist/historicist scholarship. The conventions of scholarly writing have been to write about literary texts in the present tense, thus expressing their imaginative presence, and about historical events in the past tense to mark their temporal distance from the writer who recounts them. This distinction is breaking down, both in popularized history, where the present tense is increasingly used to give a sense of immediacy to accounts of past events, and in postmodern historical theory, which is informed by the recognition that history, no less than fiction, is shaped by present interests and assumptions. The question of grammatical tense poses an especially pressing problem for new historicist literary criticism. The present tense effaces historical distance, the past denies literary presence, and the distinction between past tense for history and present tense for fiction implicitly denies the involvement of the literary text in its historical context that animates the entire new historicist project. If the text and its historical context are components of a seamless discursive web, it is difficult to sustain the grammatical distinction between present and past tenses that marks the separation of literary text from its historical context. But if that distinction is elided, where does the new historicist scholar situate herself in relation to the literary/historical objects of her analysis? Using the present tense, as Erickson does in the passage I quoted, seems to claim universal validity for a historically situated response. At the same time, however, it also seems to acknowledge that the version of past experience being constructed is a projection of current interests and anxieties.

The present tense is also the conventional form for references to the work of other scholars, as if it too existed in a timeless, ahistorical space. As we all know, however, scholarly texts, no less than the texts scholars study, are imbricated in the historical contexts in which they were produced and shaped by the social locations and personal interests and desires of their writers, even though the conventions of academic civility make those factors difficult to discuss. Nonetheless, I believe it is important to note, not only that the feminist/historicist Shakespeare criticism of the 1980s often tended to privilege male experience, emphasizing masculine anxiety in the face of powerful women, but also that some of the most influential work of that period was, in fact, produced by male critics.

One of the best-known modern readings of *As You Like It*, for instance, Louis Adrian Montrose's 1981 article, 'The Place of a Brother', proposed to reverse the then prevailing view of the play by arguing that 'what happens to Orlando at home is not Shakespeare's contrivance to get him into the forest; what happens to Orlando in the forest is Shakespeare's contrivance to remedy what has happened to him at home'.[21] Just as Oliver has displaced Orlando from his rightful place in the patriarchy, Montrose's reading displaces Rosalind from her place as the play's protagonist, focusing instead upon the relationships among brothers, fathers, and sons. Although Oliver appears only briefly on stage and the brothers' reconciliation is narrated, not shown, the main issue in the play is said to be Orlando's troubled relationship with his brother and consequent loss of his rightful place in society. Rosalind is reduced to a vehicle for its restoration: marrying her enables Orlando to become 'heir apparent to the reinstated Duke' (p. 38). Montrose does not cite Gayle Rubin's 1975 article 'The Traffic in Women', but this is the paradigm that seems to lie behind his argument.[22] The power of Rubin's anthropological analysis of the ways women are exchanged in marriage in order to secure bonds between the men (usually fathers) who bestow them and the husbands to whom they are given is so great that it supersedes the evidence of the play in Montrose's argument. In performance, Rosalind clearly dominates the action (she has the longest part, speaking, according to the Spevack *Concordance*, 26.744 per cent of the words in the playscript). The scenes in the forest, where four pairs of lovers court, quarrel, and marry, take up most of the playing time. Most important, Rosalind's marriage to Orlando is motivated not by her father's wishes but by her own long-standing desire. She falls in love with Orlando the first time she sees him, and when Celia asks her whether she is thinking about her banished father ('is all this for your father?'), her reply, 'No, some of it is for my child's father' (1.3.8–10) indicates that she is already planning to marry him. Moreover, when they finally do prepare to marry, it is Rosalind, not her father, who tells Orlando 'To you I give myself' (5.4.106). In fact, none of the marriages in the play is arranged by a father. The only marriage that can be said to be arranged is that of Silvius and Phoebe, which Rosalind herself arranges. Nonetheless, Montrose's argument that the play 'is a structure for her containment' (p. 52) has been widely influential in subsequent criticism.

With the turn to history in literary studies generally, and especially in the field of the Renaissance, feminist Shakespeare criticism has been almost completely shaped by the scholarly consensus about the pervasiveness of masculine anxiety and women's disempowerment in Shakespeare's world. Much of this criticism is sympathetic to women's plights, exposing women's oppression and describing the sociological, psychological, and ideological mechanisms that produced it, but it poses problems that are simultaneously intellectual and political. Feminist scholarship needs history, and it needs the analytic instruments the new historicism provides. The problem is that the conceptual categories that shape contemporary scholarly discourse, no less than the historical records of the past, are often man-made and shaped by men's anxieties, desires, and interests. As such, they constitute instruments of women's exclusion, and often of women's oppression. What Kathleen McLuskie wrote about *Measure for Measure* in 1985 seems increasingly applicable to the entire Shakespearian canon and to historical accounts of the world in which he wrote: 'Feminist criticism', she argued, 'is restricted to exposing its own exclusion from the text. It has no point of entry into it, for the dilemmas of the narrative and the sexuality under discussion are constructed in completely male terms.'[23] How then can we enter the discourse of current feminist/historicist Shakespeare criticism without becoming so thoroughly inscribed within its categories that we are forced to imagine both the plays and the culture in which they were produced from a male point of view?

It is important to remember that feminist criticism began with a political agenda, although—especially in the United States—it has increasingly entered the mainstream of academic discourse. The current interest in issues of sex and gender has provided increased academic visibility for feminist concerns and increased professional visibility for academic feminists, but this has not come without costs. Adopted as a conceptual tool by women and men without a serious commitment to feminist political agendas, criticism designated as 'feminist' has provided arguments that can just as easily be used to naturalize women's oppression as to oppose it. Among the consequences for women students of Shakespeare's plays is the fact that we are being taught to read from the subject position of a man, and a misogynist man at that. The way we read Shakespeare's plays matters because the cultural prestige of Shakespeare makes his plays a model for contemporary values and the privileged site where past history is reconstructed. Even academic historians often turn to Shakespeare for evidence of past practices and attitudes. The index to Anthony Fletcher's *Gender, Sex and Subordination in England 1500–1800*, for instance, lists fifty-four references to Shakespeare's plays. Another recent history, Beatrice Gottlieb's *The Family in the Western World from the Black Death to the Industrial Age*, frankly states that the author has chosen to 'rely mainly on Shakespeare' for evidence of 'what people thought of the emotional role of the family'.[24]

This is not to deny that there is ample evidence for a history of misogyny and of women's oppression in Shakespeare's world and that there are good reasons why it needed to be pointed out. All the statements I have cited are documented with quotations from early modern texts and citations of early modern cultural practice; and, as Lynda Boose has eloquently written in her brilliant study of *The Taming of the Shrew*, it is essential to 'assert an intertextuality that binds the obscured records of a painful women's history' to the Shakespearian text because 'that history has paid for the right to speak itself'; and 'the impulse to rewrite the more oppressively patriarchal material in this play serves the very ideologies about gender that it makes less visible by making less offensive' (pp. 181–2). However, as Boose also makes clear, although the history of male misogyny is inextricably entangled with the history of women's oppression, those histories had strikingly different consequences for women and men. In considering the evidence for Renaissance misogyny and the oppressive practices it produced, it is important to remember an essential axiom of postmodern historical study—the fact that, as Sandra Harding has wittily remarked, there is no such thing as a 'view from nowhere'. For feminists, there are obvious dangers in contemplating our past from the point of view of late twentieth-century academic men, who may—consciously or not—be anxious or ambivalent about the progress women have made in the wake of the contemporary women's movement. We need to view the textual evidence for misogyny and oppression more critically, considering both the social locations of the original writers and those of the contemporary scholars who have put those texts back into circulation.

As Deborah Payne has argued in another context, certain anecdotes, texts, and passages from texts are repeatedly cited and assumed 'to represent dominant social views . . . This "short-circuit fallacy" . . . can occur only by ignoring [the writer of the text's or the recorder of the anecdote's] vexed position within the social space' from which he writes.[25] Payne adopts the phrase *short-circuit fallacy* from Pierre Bourdieu, who defines it as ignoring 'the crucial mediation provided by . . . the field of cultural production . . . a social space with its own logic, within which agents struggle over stakes of a particular kind'. 'The most essential bias', he goes on to warn, is the ' "ethnocentrism of the scientist," which consists in ignoring everything that the analyst injects into his perception of the object by virtue of the fact that he is placed outside of the object, that he observes it from afar and from above'.[26] Carol Thomas Neely makes a similar point in a study of madness and gender in Shakespeare's tragedies and early modern culture:

The complexities of reading the discourse of madness in Shakespeare and his culture reveal the difficulty and necessity of historicizing: examining one's own position and that of one's subject(s) in contemporary culture in relation to the construction of those subject(s) which emerged in early modern culture, working to tease out disjunctions and connections. This project reveals that the shape of gender difference cannot be assumed but must always be reformulated in specific cultural and historical contexts.[27]

The lesson, in the words of Jean E. Howard's important essay on the new historicism, is that 'there is no transcendent space from which one can perceive the past "objectively" '. 'Our view', she continues, 'is always informed by our present position'.[28] It follows from this that 'objectivity is not in any pure form a possibility', that 'interpretive and even descriptive acts' are inevitably political, and that 'any move into history is [therefore] an intervention' (p. 43).

One strategy for intervention adopted by feminist scholars in the 1980s and 1990s has been to look for places within patriarchal scripts that allow opportunities for female agency. In 1981, for instance, Coppélia Kahn argued in *Man's Estate* that the power over women given to men by patriarchy made men paradoxically 'vulnerable to women' because 'a woman's subjugation to her husband's will was the measure of his patriarchal authority and thus of his manliness'.[29] In 1985, Catherine Belsey pointed out in *The Subject of Tragedy* that women convicted of witchcraft were empowered at the moment of their execution by the 'requirement for confessions from the scaffold', which 'paradoxically... offered women a place from which to speak in public with a hitherto unimagined authority which was not diminished by the fact that it was demonic'.[30] In 1994, Frances E. Dolan focused in *Dangerous Familiars* on early modern representations of domestic crimes perpetrated by women in an effort 'to uncover the possibilities, however contingent and circumscribed, for human agency in historical process', because 'accounts of domestic violence' are 'one set of scripts in which women could be cast as agents, albeit in problematic terms'.[31]

Increasingly, however, feminist scholars are challenging the patri-archal narrative itself, recovering the materials for alternative narra-tives and emphasizing that repressive prescriptions should not be regarded as descriptions of actual behaviour. The statement in the 1632 treatise *The Law's Resolutions of Women's Rights* that all women were 'understood either married or to be married' has been repeatedly cited, and it has shaped many of our assumptions about women's place in Shakespeare's world.[32] However, Amy Louise Erickson pointed out in her 1993 study of *Women and Property in Early Modern England*, that

...it is one thing to observe that early modern male writers invariably described women's place in the social hierarchy, the 'great chain of being,' entirely in terms of marriage. It is quite another to remember that they did so in a society in which most adult women in the population at any given time were not married—they were either widowed or they had never married.[33]

Similarly, despite the often-cited injunctions that women's place was confined within their husbands' homes, Diana E. Henderson reminds us in a 1997 essay that

Some aristocratic women, in fact, managed to avoid being confined to any of their numerous homes, much less 'the' home; those at the other end of the social scale might have no home at all, and they could hardly afford to create gendered space....Texts, (especially literary ones) tend to preserve the voices and perspectives of those who dominated within society; we must supplement them with both historical data and our scholarly imaginations if we wish to hear more of the conversation. Female-headed households in *Gammer Gur-ton's Needle* may be only a schoolmaster's source of comedy or deflected anxiety, but it is also true that there were many female-headed households in town and city alike; historical study of Southwark, the theater district itself, reveals that at least 16 percent of households were headed by a woman. The type of historical evidence we bring to bear when interpreting plays undoubt-edly informs what types of domesticity we see represented, what gaps we notice, how we value them.[34]

Thus, while *As You Like It* is a fantasy, the female household that Rosalind and Celia establish in the forest had precedents in the very district where the theatre was located. Moreover, Rosalind's role in arranging her own marriage, and Phoebe's as well, also had ample precedents in the real world. Early modern Englishwomen played central roles in arranging marriages, not only their own, but also those of their daughters, nieces, and granddaughters. Far more fathers than mothers had died by the time their children reached marriageable age; and even when both parents were alive, great numbers of women lived away from their parents' homes, often supporting themselves independently and negotiating their own marriages. Vivien Brodsky Elliott's study of single women in the London marriage market during the years 1598 to 1619 shows that women who had migrated from the country to work in London tended to marry later than London-born women and to marry men who were closer to their own age, statistics that, Elliott concludes, suggest 'a greater freedom of choice of spouse and a more active role for women in the courtship and marriage process': 'without the control or influence of their parents the marriage process for them was one in which they had an active role in initiating their own relationships, in finding suitable partners, and in conducting courtships'.[35] Among the upper levels of society where there was more property involved and parents were more likely to take an active role in arranging their children's marriages, Margaret Ezell's study of women's correspondence with other women reveals that mothers, grandmothers, and aunts played central roles in negotiating marriages for their children (Ezell, pp. 20–34).

Women's power and authority extended beyond the limits of their families. The example of the Tudor queens Mary and Elizabeth is well known, and the 'anomaly' of Elizabeth's position has been endlessly noted; but they were not the only women who exercised political authority. As owners of boroughs, two of the Queen's female subjects were able to choose Members of Parliament.[36] Others voted in parliamentary elections. Patricia Crawford's examination of voting registers reveals that in some parts of England, 'women had been regularly voting in parliamentary elections during the seventeenth century into the 1650s at least' (Orgel, p. 74). Since material wealth was the criterion for voting, women who were freeholders were sometimes allowed to vote along with their male counterparts (Fraser, pp. 230–1). Women also possessed considerable economic power, not only through inheritance from fathers and husbands (and from mothers and other female relatives as well), but also by virtue of their own gainful employment. Widows were usually named executrix in their husbands' wills, and when a husband died intestate, the widow was legally entitled to administer the estate (Amy Louise Erickson, pp. 19, 61–78, 175). Bess of Hardwick began with a marriage portion of forty marks, but ended, after inheriting the property of four successive husbands, as the Countess of Shrewsbury and one of the wealthiest women in England.[37] Women lower on the social scale earned their livings, not only as servants, but also in a variety of trades that took them outside the household. Itinerant chapwomen peddled a variety of goods, and Amy Louise Erickson has noted that 'prohibitions upon girls and women appearing in public places like markets and fairs are entirely absent from early modern ballads and broadsides' (p. 10). Women's prominence in the marketplace is also attested by the drawings of thirteen London food markets produced by Hugh Alley in 1598, which include numerous images of women, both alone and with other women or men, both buying and selling (see Figure 1).[38] These images are particularly significant, because Alley's text is not specifically concerned with the activities of women in the markets; the women are simply there, apparently as a matter of course.

Even the guilds, generally believed to be bastions of male privilege, included women. The Statute of Artificers referred to apprentices as 'persons'; and individual acts mentioned girls as well as boys and mistresses as well as masters: women were legally entitled, not only to enter apprenticeship but also to take on apprentices of their own.[39] As Stephen Orgel points out,

until late in the seventeenth century women, in one place or another, were admitted into practically every English trade or guild. Women did not, moreover, limit their efforts to ladylike pursuits: in Chester, in 1575, there were five women blacksmiths. Elsewhere, women were armourers, bootmakers, printers, pewterers, goldsmiths, farriers, and so forth . . . and they pursued these trades not as wives, widows, or surrogates, but as fully independent, legally responsible craftspersons. This point needs especially to be stressed, since a common modern way of ignoring the presence of women in the Renaissance workforce is to claim that they were there only as emanations of

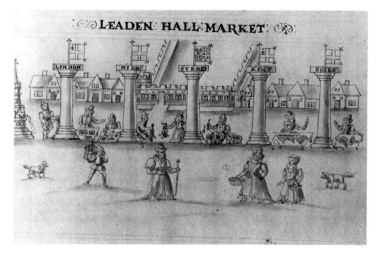

1. 'The Leaden Hall Market', from Hugh Alley, *A Caveat for the City of London* (1598)

absent or dead husbands: this is not the case. The *percentage* of female apprentices is especially notable, for a practice that [the noted historians] Lawrence Stone and E. P. Thompson believe did not exist. In Southampton, for example, at the beginning of the seventeenth century, 48 percent—almost half—the apprentices were women.[40]

The historical evidence I have sampled undermines the current scholarly consensus that respectable women were expected to stay at home, that they were economically dependent on fathers and husbands, and that they were subjected to constant surveillance by jealous men, obsessively anxious about their sexual fidelity. I found it because I was looking for it. Historical evidence, as my old teacher reminded me, is subject to selective citation and motivated interpretation. The same, of course, is true of literary texts. In a 1985 study of *King John*, I easily discovered that

Lady Falconbridge's infidelity has created the nightmare situation that haunts the patriarchal imagination—a son not of her husband's getting destined to inherit her husband's lands and title. Like Shakespeare's ubiquitous cuckold jokes, the Falconbridge episode bespeaks the anxiety that motivates the stridency of patriarchal claims and repressions.[41]

That reading seemed valid to me because it confirmed the paradigmatic view of women's place in Shakespeare's world. Looking at it now, I realize that it elided a number of features of the text: the facts that the revelation of Lady Falconbridge's adultery is depicted in humorous terms, that the Bastard it produced is a sympathetic character, that he welcomes the disclosure of his bastardy, and that it results in his acceptance as the son of Richard Coeur-de-Lion and consequent social elevation. Of course, the lady's husband, who might indeed have been jealous, is no longer alive when the revelation occurs.

Nonetheless, if we re-examine the representations of male sexual jealousy in Shakespeare's other plays, it is difficult to sustain the assumption that it expresses a normative view. Othello's jealousy of Desdemona is the source of tragedy; Leontes' jealousy of Hermione is the source of near-tragedy in *The Winter's Tale*; Ford's jealousy of his wife is the subject of comic debunking in *The Merry Wives of Windsor*. And all are mistaken. To be sure, Shakespeare does depict unfaithful wives. Goneril in *King Lear* and Margaret in the *Henry VI* plays are obvious examples. But it is worth noting that in neither case is the woman's infidelity her only, or even her chief, offence; and neither husband is wracked by jealousy. In other plays of the period, unfaithful wives are forgiven. Sometimes, in fact, their infidelity goes undetected. Consider, for instance, the case of Winnifride in William Rowley, Thomas Dekker, and John Ford's play *The Witch of Edmonton* (1621): she is pregnant by another man when she marries Frank Thorney, who believes the baby is his. Never punished for her transgression, she is depicted throughout in sympathetic terms and, at the end of the play, is welcomed into the home of the supremely virtuous Carters. Sir Arthur Clarington, the cold-hearted aristocrat who seduced Winnifride when she was his maidservant, is denounced as 'the instrument that wrought all' the 'misfortunes' of the other characters (5.2.1–3). According to Old Carter, he is 'worthier to be hang'd' than Frank Thorney, who murdered Carter's daughter (5.2.7–8).[42]

In attempting to interpret the plays of Shakespeare and his contemporaries historically, probably the best starting place for a feminist critic is Jean E. Howard's reminder that women were paying customers in early modern theatres.[43] According to the records of early English playgoers compiled by Andrew Gurr, these included respectable women, such as the wife of John Overall, who was Regius Professor of Theology at Cambridge from 1596 to 1607 and Dean of St Paul's from 1602 to 1618 (p. 207). In fact, Gurr found far more references to citizens' wives and ladies than to whores (p. 62), even though references to prostitutes seeking customers are more familiar to modern readers whose assumptions about the women in the playhouses have been shaped by scholarly citations of antitheatrical literature. Those assumptions were not, apparently, shared by the players, who explicitly defer to female playgoers in prologues and epilogues. The Epilogue to Shakespeare's *Henry VIII* expects to hear 'good' about the play 'only in | The merciful construction of good women, | For such a one we showed 'em', acknowledging that positive representations of female characters were likely to appeal to female playgoers. In *The Knight of the Burning Pestle*, a citizen and his wife repeatedly interrupt the players to demand changes in the represented action, and, although both are the subjects of satire, there is no suggestion that her interruptions are more inappropriate than his because she is a woman or that her husband's wishes are to be honoured more than hers. Ben Jonson, whom it would be difficult to accuse of excessive deference to women, dedicated *The Alchemist* to Lady Mary Wroth, and declared in the Prologue to *Epicoene* his intention to provide a dramatic feast 'fit for ladies . . . lords, knights, squires, . . . your waiting-wench and city-wires [i.e. citizens' wives who wore fashionable ruffs supported by wires], . . . your men, and daughters of Whitefriars'. Jonson's assumption that women's interests might be different from men's and that both needed to be pleased is supported by no less a personage than Queen Anne, who not only patronized two companies of players (The Children of the Queen's Revels and Queen Anne's Men) but also, according to the French ambassador, attended plays in which 'the comedians of the metropolis bring [King James] upon the stage'. The Queen, the ambassador reported, 'attends these representations in order to enjoy the laugh against her husband'.[44]

It is generally assumed that private playhouse audiences were more homogeneous than those in the large, public amphitheatres like Shakespeare's Globe, but even the private playhouses catered to women as well as men, and, as these examples show, those women came into the playhouses with tastes, interests, and allegiances that were not necessarily the same as men's. Moreover, it is difficult to imagine a totalizing master narrative that would account for the varied experiences, tastes, interests, and allegiances of all the women who enjoyed playgoing in Shakespeare's England. They included applewives and fishwives, doxies and respectable citizens, queens and great ladies (Gurr, pp. 60–4). Because playing was a commercial enterprise, it was in the players' interests to please as many of the paying customers as they could, the women no less than the men. The female playgoers in Shakespeare's London brought their own per-spectives to the action. Perhaps we should try harder to emulate their example. Women were everywhere in Shakespeare's England, but the variety of their roles in life and in the scripts of plays too often goes without notice. If we wanted to look for it, I think we could find an interpretive embarrassment of riches for a revitalized feminist criticism.

The Place(s) of Women in Shakespeare's World: Historical Fact and Feminist Interpretation

Recent feminist Shakespeare scholarship has relied heavily on historical accounts of the place of women in Shakespeare's world, which is often invoked to ground interpretations of the playscripts in a foundation of historical fact. Nonetheless, it is important to remember that, as I argued in the Introduction, historical writing itself is a kind of story-telling. The reconstruction of past lives is finally an impossible task, compromised by the distance and difference that separate the history-writing present from the historical past it seeks to know. We look to the past to discover answers to the questions that trouble us here and now, but no matter how hard we struggle to recover the past as it really was, the questions we ask are the products of our own concerns, the answers we find, even when couched in the words of old texts, the products of our own selection and arrangement.

These difficulties are especially troublesome in the case of women. There are far fewer historical records of women than of men, and the questions with which modern historians approach the records that have been found are heavily fraught with present concerns and present controversies. On the one hand, because the experience of women tends to be occluded in the historical record, there is the temptation to universalize—to assume that the essential aspects of women's experience were always and everywhere what they are now and here. On the other hand, because the history of women's struggle for equality during the last two centuries is relatively well documented, studies of women's history often construct a meliorist narrative in which the progress women have made in recent times represents the final stage in a long upward trajectory. The radical incompleteness of the historical record has made both assumptions plausible, but neither is the only story that can be woven around the evidence we have. And because both stories have been told so often in recent years, it seems to me that the most useful project at present is to challenge both the pessimistic conviction that the essential aspects of women's experience have remained relatively unchanged and the optimistic contrast between past oppression and present opportunity.

I cannot hope to recreate the lives of the actual women Shakespeare knew—or even to recover most of their names. What I can do, however, is to bring together some of the materials that emphasize the ways the practices and beliefs that informed Shakespeare's experiences of women differed from our own and also challenge the story of female oppression and disempowerment that is often told in recent accounts of women's place in Shakespeare's England. In Shakespeare's world, inequalities between men and women were taken for granted. Sanctioned by law and religion and reinforced by the duties and customs of daily life, they were deeply embedded in the fabric of culture. However, the gender hierarchy in Shakespeare's time coexisted with a hierarchy of status and rank, which was also rationalized by theology, and by history as well. The hierarchy of status and rank was just as firmly embedded as the gender hierarchy, and, like the gender hierarchy, it was sanctioned by law and religion and reinforced by customary behaviour. As a result, the fact that male superiority was taken for granted does not mean that every woman was subordinate in every way to every man or that many women did not occupy positions of authority and power that would be considered exceptional even today. The easy assumption of a broad, schematic opposition between past oppression and present equality ignores the variety, the complexity, and the contradictions of women's positions in our own world, not to mention those of a remote—and finally inaccessible—past.

Myriad distinctions of status, geography, religion, and occupation determined the social positions, opportunities, wealth, and power available to individual women in Shakespeare's England. Moreover, as Raymond Williams has argued, the dominant features of a culture always coexist both with residual 'elements of the past' and with 'emergent' elements that are in the process of 'being created'.[1] Unlike our own conceptions of gender differences, for instance, male superiority was rationalized less in the then relatively marginal discourse of the new biological science than in the established and privileged discourse of theology. Nonetheless, even in Shakespeare's plays, anticipations of the biologically grounded ideology of compulsory heterosexuality that authorizes the modern nuclear family can be found in plays that focus on the life of the proto-bourgeoisie. In *The Taming of the Shrew*, for instance, Kate's final speech rationalizes the submission of wives to husbands not only on the traditional analogy between husband and king ('Such duty as the subject owes the prince, | Even such a woman oweth to her husband'), but also on the now-familiar ground of the physical differences between male and female bodies ('Why are our bodies soft, and weak, and smooth, | ... But that our soft conditions and our hearts | Should well agree with our external parts?'). In a time of rapid cultural change, the places of women in families, in the economy, in religion, and in popular thinking were undergoing equally radical transformations. Renaissance texts contain anticipations of modern constructions of gender and sexuality as well as vestiges of medieval ones, just as vestiges of earlier formulations persist in our own discourse.

Clothing offers a good example of the ways gendered identity was complicated by all these factors. In sixteenth-century England, as in our own culture, women's clothing was clearly distinguished from men's. Until the late Middle Ages, however, men and women had worn similar long, loose robes. During the fourteenth and fifteenth centuries, clothing had been increasingly differentiated to emphasize and produce embodied sexual difference. Men's robes were shortened to reveal their legs, and the codpiece was invented. Women acquired tight bodices that altered the shape of their breasts and low-cut gowns to display them, and their skirts, which remained long, were widened. In addition to producing visible signs of sexual difference, changes in clothing also produced differences in daily behaviour. It was during this same period, for instance, that European women began using sidesaddles, a fashion that was brought to England near the end of the fourteenth century by Anne of Bohemia when she married the

English king Richard II.[2] However, gender was not the only or even the most important distinction that early modern English clothing enforced. In fact, although sumptuary laws contained elaborate regulations of male attire to ensure that men's clothing would express their exact place in the social hierarchy, there was no legislation against cross-dressing. In late sixteenth- and early seventeenth-century England, some women adopted the fashion of masculine attire, and although moralists strenuously condemned the practice, it was never made illegal. Moreover, male and female children were dressed in the same attire—in skirts—until they reached the age of seven. Apparently, the physical difference that separated boys from girls was not considered sufficiently significant to be marked by clothing, but the difference in social rank that separated one man from another was so important that clothing which obscured it was forbidden by law. Another indication that both age and status were at least as important as gender in determining an individual's identity is the fact that medical casebooks referred to children of both sexes as 'it' until they reached puberty. In our own culture, by contrast, clothing is gendered from birth, but it is less reliable as an indicator of status and rank. Heads of state appear on television dressed in blue jeans, and American teenagers from working-class families wear full formal regalia to their high-school proms. Our children, however, are wrapped in pink or blue blankets even in hospital nurseries, insisting on the innate, biological difference between male and female while eliding the still-present distinctions of status and privilege that the egalitarian ideology of modern Western democracy denies.

Political leadership is another example of the ways the status hierarchy—and religious allegiance as well—complicated the relative positions of men and women in ways that are difficult to understand in modern terms. At the time of Shakespeare's birth in 1564, women—first Queen Mary and then Queen Elizabeth—had already occupied the English throne for eleven years, and Elizabeth was to reign for most of his adult life. Reluctance to accept women in positions of power has kept women from ever holding the presidency of the United States, and even from being nominated for that office by a major political party, but it is rarely expressed so vehemently as it was by John Knox in his *First Blast of the Trumpet against the Monstrous Regiment of Women*, which was published in 1558. Knox argued that any authority held by a woman above a man was a monstrous usurpation, forbidden by God, repellent to nature, and condemned by ancient authorities. It is important to remember, however, that Knox's diatribe, written in exile in Geneva, was in fact directed against Mary Tudor and the other Catholic queens who were governing in France and Scotland. Only a few months after the publication of Knox's *First Blast*, Mary Tudor died, and her Protestant sister Elizabeth ascended the English throne. Once that happened, as J. E. Neale trenchantly observed,

The Protestant fraternity, Knox included, were only too ready, now that a Deborah [i.e. Elizabeth] was on the English throne, to cease blowing this trumpet; and as the Catholics, if they were to favour an alternative ruler, must likewise look to a woman [i.e. Mary Queen of Scots], Elizabeth was not likely to be disturbed by theories about the legitimacy of female rule.[3]

As Neale recognized, in this case, religion was a far more important issue than gender to both Elizabeth's supporters and her enemies. The religious allegiances of the Shakespeare family have long been a subject of debate, although some scholars have recently mounted impressive arguments that William was brought up as a Catholic. Even if that proves to be so, however, it is important to remember that the vast majority of English Catholics remained loyal to their Queen and country.

Queen Elizabeth brought exceptional political skills to her office, and during the years when Shakespeare was growing up, she was consolidating her remarkable and unprecedented popularity among the vast majority of her subjects. Every year on 17 November, the Queen's accession was celebrated with the ringing of church bells, sermons of thanksgiving, and public festivities. These celebrations reflected the widespread popular devotion to the Queen, which intensified after the defeat of the Northern rebellion of 1569. Hundreds of records of local celebrations in churchwardens' accounts corroborate Thomas Holland's claim in a 1599 sermon that the Accession Day celebrations 'flowed by a voluntary current all over this Realm'.[4]

Queen Elizabeth actively courted her subjects with annual royal progresses through the countryside. She rode on horseback or in an open litter so the people who lined the roads could see and speak directly with their monarch during these slow processions. In 1575 the court poet Thomas Churchyard described her enthusiastic greeting by the city of Bristol:

> No sooner was pronounced the name,
>   but babes in street gan leap:
> The youth, the age, the rich, the poor,
>   came running all on heap,
> And clapping hands, cried mainly out,
>   O blessed be the hour:
> Our Queen is coming to the town,
>   with princely train and power.
> Then colours cast they over the walls,
>   and decked old houses gay:[5]

Written to be recited to the Queen when she entered the town by a boy dressed as Fame, Churchyard's enthusiastic description can be taken with a grain of salt, but it is only one of the many contemporary accounts of Queen Elizabeth's remarkable popularity among the common people of England. According to a 1569 report by the Spanish ambassador, for instance, 'She was received everywhere with great acclamations and signs of joy.... She ordered her carriage sometimes to be taken where the crowd seemed thickest, and stood up and thanked the people' (Neale, pp. 211–12).

A modern historian of the Tudor dynasty concludes his book with a similarly enthusiastic tribute:

There can be no docketing or summarising of Queen Elizabeth.... In the year of the Armada the Pope himself said 'She is a great woman; and were she only Catholic she would be without her match.' Certainly, among all English sovereigns, no others ... have impressed themselves so indelibly upon the popular memory and imagination. It was not for nothing that November 17th, the date of her accession, was a national holiday for two hundred years. Nor is it a wonder that in 1589 a forgotten Westminster schoolboy called John Slye, whose dog-eared text of Caesar has been discovered in an Oxford library, should have scribbled in the margins some doggerel that would be a little odd from a schoolboy in any other period.

> The rose is red, the leaves are green.

> God save Elizabeth, our noble Queen.

He scribbled profusely all over the book, but what occurs most often is the single word 'Elizabeth'.[6]

In stark contrast, most recent scholarship on Queen Elizabeth insists on the difficulties she encountered as a woman in a position of authority over men and emphasizes evidence that seems to indicate that her male subjects experienced anxieties similar to those expressed by the scholars' own contemporaries in the wake of the modern women's movement. Recent work on the politics of the Elizabethan court, for instance, tends to assume the viewpoint of male courtiers, emphasizing their discomfort in service to a female ruler. However, the semi-public spaces of her court, such as the privy chamber and the presence chamber in which male courtiers predominated, were not the only political arenas in which the Queen held sway. Although she was served in her private apartments (withdrawing chambers) by maids of honour and ladies of the bedchamber, 'the *noblewoman* or lady-in-waiting', as Philippa Berry points out, is usually 'elided from contemporary critical views of the Elizabethan court'.[7] Other elisions from recent accounts of Elizabeth's reign include her remarkable popularity among the vast majority of her subjects and the contemporary accounts of the admiration for the effectiveness of her rule expressed by foreign rulers, for whom similarities between their problems as monarchs were more significant than their differences as man and woman. Essex, for instance, has elicited considerable sympathy from recent historians of Elizabeth's reign, and the story of his rebellion and the events that led up to it is usually told from his own point of view. It is important to remember, however, that the rebellion failed to attract the popular support that Essex anticipated. Contrary to his hopes and expectations, the citizens of London did not join his revolt, and many of his own followers deserted him as soon as he was denounced as a traitor. Even in France, 'there was great admiration for the courage and resolution with which Elizabeth had handled the Essex rising. Would that their King Henry III had had but a part of her spirit to quell the insolency of the Duke of Guise on the Day of Barricades! "She only is a king!" exclaimed Henry IV. "She only knows how to rule!" ' (Neale, p. 393). Of all the rulers of her time in Western Europe, she was the only one able to deal with the issue of religious conflict. In the judgement of the historian Richard S. Dunn, 'This achievement alone is a good reason for nominating Elizabeth the ablest politician of her time'.[8]

Mountains of evidence have been adduced in support of both accounts of Elizabeth's reign—the older and more popular emphasis on her remarkable success as a monarch and the recent scholarly emphasis upon the disabilities produced by her gender that haunted her entire reign. Evidence about the ordinary women Shakespeare would have known as a boy in Stratford-upon-Avon is harder to come by; but in this case as well, alternative descriptions can be constructed. Scholarly accounts of Shakespeare's youth and family focus on men, such as his father and schoolmaster, partly because of the greater visibility of men in the surviving records, and probably also because of the modern scholars' own greater interest in their activities. Thus, for instance, a glance at the indexes to two standard biographies of Shakespeare shows respectively twenty-six and twenty-seven entries referring to his father but only twelve and fourteen for his mother.[9] The preponderance of men in the documentary records that have been discovered and cited may, however, be misleading. Because most of the women in Shakespeare's family outlived their brothers and husbands, the family in which he grew up was actually predominantly female. In addition to numerous sisters and female cousins, Shakespeare had eight aunts, including one who outlived her husband by forty-one years.[10]

Sixteenth-century legal records show that the women in Shakespeare's family controlled considerable property both in land and in money. They also bequeathed property, served as executors of wills, and engaged in litigation designed to defend and further their financial interests. Shakespeare's mother, for instance, although she had nine older sisters and two older brothers, inherited the only freehold property her father bequeathed and served as one of his two executors.[11] This was not exceptional. In fact, most of the executors of wills in Shakespeare's England were women rather than men—so much so that scribes sometimes mistakenly used the female form 'executrix' to refer to male executors of wills.[12] Among the many other women in and around Stratford who served as executors for their fathers' or husbands' wills were Joan Hathaway, the stepmother of William Shakespeare's wife, and Margaret Sadler, the sister of his neighbour and lifelong friend Hamnet Sadler.

Like most of the other women in Shakespeare's family, his mother outlived her husband, but Mary Shakespeare must have had considerable authority in the household even during the years when her husband was still living and her son William was growing up. As a woman, her legal status was subordinate to her husband's, but as Robert Arden's heiress, her social status was distinctly superior. John Shakespeare was eventually to rise to the office of bailiff in Stratford, a position of considerable importance, since a bailiff was one of the aldermen who governed the town, elected by the other aldermen in consultation with the lord of the manor to serve a one-year term in an office similar to the modern positions of mayor and justice of the peace. However, he began life as the son of a tenant farmer, and Mary was the daughter of John's landlord, Robert Arden. A substantial property owner, Mary's father also possessed an ancient and respected family name. Evidence that Mary's inherited status was important to John, and to his son William as well, can be found in the documentary records of John's attempts, beginning when William was only five years old, to acquire a coat of arms. This project did not succeed for over twenty years, and it is likely that it was finally brought to a successful conclusion by William, who was by then a successful playwright in London. Significantly, one of the arguments cited in favour of the grant was that 'John had maryed the daughter & one of the heyres of Robert Arden of Wilmcoote in the said Counte, esquire'. In 1599, John or William made a further request to the heralds that the Shakespeares be permitted to impale the arms of the Arden family with their own.

In addition to her inherited status as Robert Arden's daughter, Mary was an active participant in the economic life of the household. Some of this participation can be documented from legal records concerning the sale and conveyance of various pieces of property and litigation about it in which Mary's name appears along with her husband's. Most of it can only be inferred from what we know about the domestic responsibilities of women in Mary's position during the period, which would have been very different from those of a stereo-typical 'housewife' in a modern Western country. The sexual division of labour and the conceptual division between 'public' and 'private' spheres of activity that define the positions of 'housewives' in advanced industrial nations were accepted only slowly and with difficulty in pre-capitalist England. The household had not yet been limited and specialized to its modern status as a residential unit.

Instead, it was the site where much of the economic production of the nation was conducted—the place where families not only lived together but worked together as well in a great variety of trades. They were weavers and knitters, bakers and butchers, tailors and grocers, printers, turners, merchants, and innkeepers—and this is by no means a comprehensive list. Moreover, because it was customary for workers to live on the premises, the members of a household were not restricted to kin. In a farming family, there would be hired agricultural labourers, both male and female, who worked both in and outside the house. Like their mistresses, female agricultural workers were expected not only to cook and to help with the dairying, but also to care for animals and to work in the fields. The young unmarried men and women who were employed as apprentices and servants in all these households were also involved in domestic work. One important consequence of these living arrangements was that men as well as women, hired workers as well as fathers, spent time with children and were involved in their training and education. John and Mary Shakespeare's household, with the glover's workshop adjacent to the living quarters, was probably no exception.

One reason why the sexual division of labour that is now regarded as traditional was not yet practicable in most English households was that women, no less than men, were expected to provide for their own needs and to contribute to the economic well-being of their families, not only by the money and property they brought into marriage but also by managing their households and by marketing the products of their domestic labour. Married women also supported themselves and helped to support their families by remunerative labour in a variety of crafts and trades, including some that would now be considered masculine preserves. Among the trades to which women were apprenticed during the sixteenth and seventeenth centuries were those of carpenter, plumber, cordwainer, silversmith, housepainter, pipemaker, and whittawer (i.e. dresser of light leather, the same trade practised by John Shakespeare).

The most frequently mentioned trade for women, however, was housewifery. The Puritan preacher Henry Smith ended his 1591 treatise, *A Preparative to Marriage*, with the argument that, 'we call the wife *housewife*, that is house wife, not a street wife like Tamar (Gen. 38: 14), nor a field wife like Dinah (Gen. 34: 1), but a house wife, to show that a good wife keeps her house'. Smith's exhortation seems to anticipate the repressive modern ideal of the suburban, middle-class wife, confined within the four walls of a gleaming little house where she spends her days cooking and cleaning and tending to the needs of her husband and children. It is important to remember, however, that the title of 'housewife' in sixteenth-century England was not restricted to wives, but instead designated a skill to which a girl could be apprenticed. In Salisbury, for instance, Elizabeth Deacon was apprenticed in 1612 to the 'mystery and science of house-wifery and flaxdressing', and during that same year Mary Gunter was apprenticed in 'le housewifery and knitting'.[13] In fact, as Amy Louise Erickson points out, 'The title of housewife expressed a relationship to the house, rather than a necessary marital status' (p. 53). The title page of Gervase Markham's popular handbook indicates the range of skills involved in housewifery. Published in 1615, the book was entitled *The English Housewife, Containing, The inward and outward virtues which ought to be in a complete woman, As her skill in Physic, Cookery, Banqueting-stuff, Distillation, Perfumes, Wool, Hemp, Flax, Dairies, Brewing, Baking, and all other things belonging to an Household. A Work very profitable and necessary, gathered for the general good of this kingdom.* Markham's ambitious conception of a housewife's duties was not exceptional. In 1555, for instance, Sir Anthony Fitzherbert had similarly described the duties of a housewife in his *Book of Husbandry.* According to Fitzherbert, these included milking cows, taking corn and malt to the mill and making sure that the miller returned fair measure to her, baking and brewing, feeding pigs and tending fowl, growing a kitchen garden, making hay, shearing and winnowing grain, growing and processing flax and hemp, spinning and weaving, going to market 'to sell butter, cheese, milk, eggs, chickens, capons, hens, pigs, geese, and all manner of corn'. 'If she have no wool of her own', Fitzherbert advises, 'she may take wool to spin of cloth makers, and by that means she may have a convenient living' (quoted in Clark, pp. 46–9). Women at higher levels of the social hierarchy would have been equally busy. The diary of Lady Margaret Hoby for the years 1599 to 1605, for instance, shows her collecting rents, reviewing accounts, and paying bills as well as preparing food and medicines, providing for guests, and attending to the sick.[14]

There has been no end of speculation about the circumstances of Shakespeare's marriage to Anne Hathaway. At eighteen, Shakespeare was unusually young to marry, and Anne, at twenty-six or twenty-seven, was approximately eight years older. The records concerning the marriage are well known. It took place at the end of November, by special licence, which required only one reading, rather than the customary three, of banns in church and thus permitted the couple to marry before Advent, when weddings were prohibited. The birth of their first child the following May appears to be the reason for their haste. However, neither the bride's pregnancy nor her age was as exceptional as some modern scholars have supposed. Bridal pregnancy was widely tolerated during the period, and the mean marriage ages for women ranged between twenty-three and twenty-five. William and Anne Shakespeare's daughter Judith would be thirty-one years old when she married the twenty-six-year-old Thomas Quiney (Neely, p. 120).

In the case of William's marriage to Anne, as in that of the marriage of John Shakespeare to Mary Arden, it is important to remember that the choice of a spouse was not simply the fulfilment of a romantic inclination but also the basis for the establishment of an economically viable household. Both men and women took serious account of financial considerations when negotiating their marriages. Many examples survive in legal records. In 1566, for instance, Mary Baldrye told John Turner that before deciding whether to marry him, 'she would go first and see his lands and house and as she liked them so would she do'. In 1579, a Suffolk woman, Joanna Mors, agreed to marry Edward Cleve on condition that he enter a bond with her that he was worth 100 marks; and in 1572, when Christopher Pamplyn proposed marriage to Susan Mychells of Norwich, she refused to answer until she could verify that he had 'an office worth £40 a year and £110 in ready money—even though he had promised her a jointure of £10 a year'.[15] Moreover, in many respects, Shakespeare's choice of a wife was similar to his father's. Anne Hathaway was the daughter of a substantial local farmer, who had had previous business dealings with William's father, John. Like Mary, Anne must have chosen her husband without parental advice, since her parents, like Mary's, had died by the time she married. And although her inheritance was by no means comparable to Mary's, Anne was also remembered by her father in his will, which left her ten marks to be paid on the day of her marriage.

If the records of Shakespeare's mother's life are scanty, those for his wife are almost non-existent. Aside from her marriage, the baptism of her children, the meagre bequest of a second-best bed in her husband's will, and her own death, there is only the will of her father's shepherd, Thomas Whittington, who bequeathed to the poor people of Stratford forty shillings 'that is in the hand of Anne Shaxspere, Wyf unto mr. Wyllyam Shaxspere, and is due dett unto me beyng payd to myne executor by the sayd Wyllyam Shaxspere or his assigns accordyng to the true meanyng of this my wyll' (Schoenbaum, pp. 66–9). There is no evidence that Anne ever went to London with her husband or participated in any way in the theatrical business in which he made his fortune. Her name never appears on the legal records of his business dealings there. During the long periods when he was away, it would have been normal for Anne to manage the Shakespeare household in Stratford, but her name does not appear in the surviving records of her husband's business dealings in Stratford. The only clue to Anne's role in the household comes from the Latin epitaph on her gravestone, probably commissioned by one of her daughters, which begins, 'Thou, my mother, gave me life, thy breast and milk; alas! for such great bounty to me I shall give thee a tomb'. In Anne Shakespeare's time, most women who could afford to do so used wetnurses, and maternal breastfeeding was regarded as an extraordinary sign of devotion, worthy to be commemorated on a tombstone.

One way to explain Anne's absence from all of the legal documents generated by William Shakespeare's increasing prosperity—his acquisition of property, his legal and financial dealings in both Stratford and London—is the fact that common law regarded a married woman as a *feme covert*, whose legal identity was subsumed by her husband's and whose property came under his control unless it was specifically protected by a marriage settlement. However, the common-law assumption of coverture was subject to modification by a great variety of circumstances, including the applications of local manorial customs and of ecclesiastical laws (A. L. Erickson, pp. 21–45). As we have seen, married women in the neighbourhood of Stratford did control considerable property in Anne's time, and they also engaged in litigation to defend and further their financial interests. Another possible inference is that Anne's exclusion was the result of her husband's deliberate choice. When Shakespeare purchased the Blackfriars Gate-House in 1613, for instance, the indenture named three co-purchasers or trustees, even though Shakespeare himself was to be the sole owner, a legal fiction which may have been designed to prevent Anne from claiming her common-law right as a widow to a life estate in one third of her husband's lands. Similarly, a last-minute addition to Shakespeare's will suggests a deliberate effort to limit Anne's rights to his property in Stratford. In the provision that bequeaths their Stratford home, New Place, and its contents to his daughter Susanna, the following phrase was added: 'for better enabling of her to perform this my will and towards the performance thereof'. The inserted phrase, which may have been designed to prevent Anne, who would continue to reside at New Place, from interfering with Susanna's bequest, may also have been motivated by William's hostility to Anne.

Another possibility is that William did not trust Anne to manage the family property. Her absence from the legal records of all William's financial affairs might mean that Anne had an exceptionally passive role in the economic affairs of the Shakespeare family. Taken together with the testament to her maternal breastfeeding, Anne's absence from the legal records may mean that William Shakespeare's household represented a further stage than his father's—and also further than the norm—in the transformation of the English household into the feminized enclosure that it was to become in later years.

In many ways, the position of English women was deteriorating during the sixteenth and seventeenth centuries. This is not to say that women's status and opportunities had been equal to those of men during the Middle Ages, but a multitude of factors, religious, economic, and political, were now producing a widening division between public and private life and an increasing domestication of women and circumscription of their economic scope. Women's work was increasingly distinguished from men's as women were excluded from crafts and trades in which their predecessors had been active. The household was redefined as a private, feminized space, separated from the public arenas of economic and political activity, and women were increasingly confined within the rising barriers that marked its separation.

These changes were rationalized and encouraged by Puritan preachers, who argued that the primary duty of a wife was not economic production but the nurturing of children. Accordingly, they attempted to discourage the widespread practice of wetnursing on the grounds that maternal breastfeeding was required by God and nature alike. William Gouge (1578–1653) states this view forcefully in his 1622 treatise on *Domesticall Duties*, in which he anticipates and answers every possible objection to maternal nursing. Given the still prevalent assumption that married women had economic responsibilities, it is not surprising that one of the objections Gouge anticipates deals with the economic value of a mother's non-maternal labour:

A mother that hath a trade, or that hath the care of an house, will neglect much business by nursing her child, and her husband will save more by giving half a crown a week to a nurse, than if his wife gave the child suck.

Gouge, however, insists that the God-given duty to nurse takes precedence:

No outward business appertaining to a mother can be more acceptable to God than the nursing of her child. This is the most proper work of her special calling; therefore all other businesses must give place to this, and this must not be left for any other business. As for the husband saving by putting the child forth to nurse, no gain may give dispensation against a bounden duty.

Even in the seventeenth century, however, Gouge's extreme views on women's subordination were by no means typical. Although they are often quoted by modern scholars, and although Gouge was a popular preacher, the women of his own congregation criticized his restrictive interpretations of their property rights within marriage, forcing Gouge to modify them in his dedicatory epistle, where he admits,

I remember that when these Domestical Duties were first uttered out of the pulpit, much exception was taken against the application of a wife's subjection to the restraining of her from disposing the common goods of the family without, or against her husband's consent.

He then enumerates an impressive list of exceptions. None of the restrictions, he now insists, were intended to apply to the proper goods of a wife, no nor overstrictly to such goods as are set apart for the use of the family, nor to extraordinary cases, nor always to an express consent nor to the consent of such husbands as are impotent, or far and long absent. If any other warrantable caution shall be showed me, I will be as willing to admit it as any of these. Now that my meaning may not still be perverted, I pray you, in reading the restraint of wives' power in disposing the goods of the family, ever bear in mind those cautions.

As Natasha Korda observes, 'Considering the flexibility of those allowed exceptions, we may surmise that Gouge's rule was honored more often in the breach than in the observance'.[16]

In addition to the women in his family, the boy Shakespeare would have seen women presiding over other households, buying and selling in the local market and working on farms. He would also have seen women performing in theatrical entertainments. It is not known exactly when Shakespeare began his career in the London theatre, but theatrical performances of many sorts were a regular feature of life in Stratford. About a week before William and Anne Shakespeare's first child was baptized, for instance, the Stratford aldermen paid Davy Jones, who was probably related by marriage to Anne, for a Whitsun performance by his troupe of players. Stratford was a weekly market town, and it also had two licensed annual fairs, which would have included theatrical performances. Professional acting companies regularly toured the country, as they had done for hundreds of years. Between 1569, the year when John Shakespeare was bailiff, and 1587, the year when many scholars believe William Shakespeare left Stratford, local parish records list payments to nineteen companies (Thomson, p. 7). Records of payments indicate that both the Queen's Men and the Earl of Worcester's Men played during John Shakespeare's term as bailiff in 1569. The names of individual actors in those companies rarely appear in the documentary evidence, and as far as we know, they included no female players. Nonetheless, there were many women who performed in the guild plays, May games, and civic entertainments that were regular features of village life, and there were many women among the itinerant musicians, acrobats, and other performers who toured the English countryside.

Although the company William Shakespeare joined, like the other London-based professional companies, did not include women players, there was no legal prohibition against performances by women.

The example of Moll Frith's appearance on the stage of the Fortune Theatre in 1611, where she sang and played her lute, is well known and well documented; and Richard Madox reported in 1583 that he 'went to the theater to see a scurvie play set out al by one virgin' (Chambers I, p. 371). These examples appear to be atypical, but women were deeply involved in the off-stage activities of the professional companies in London. Susan Baskerville owned shares in Queen Anne's company and in the Red Bull, and two women—Marie Bryan and Margaret Gray—were shareholders in the second Fortune.[17] The fullest record we have of a company's day-to-day business, Philip Henslowe's *Diary*, contains numerous references to women who were directly or indirectly involved in that enterprise. Agnes, Henslowe's wife, is listed several times as lending money to actors. Henslowe was also involved in pawnbroking, a business that probably provided both costumes and properties for onstage use. Over three-quarters of the customers he listed were women, as were three of the four agents he named as assisting him in this business: Goody Watson, Mrs. Grant, and Ann No[c]kes. These entries are significant because costumes represented the chief stock-in-trade of the acting companies. Purchasing a new play, for instance, usually cost about £6, while a single costume could cost over three times as much.[18] As Natasha Korda has shown, women dominated the business that provided those costumes. Two of their names survive in Henslowe's *Diary*, which records payments to 'Mrs. Gosson' for making 'head-tyers', and to 'Mrs. Calle' for 'hed tyers for the corte'. References to a 'tyrewoman' also appear in the 1608 agreement of the Whitefriars playhouse housekeepers, and they are also mentioned in *The Actors Remonstrance* (1644) and the Salisbury Court Papers (1639).[19]

In addition to these offstage activities, women also participated in the business of the theatrical companies as gatherers or box-holders. Standing at the doors to collect entrance fees from the playgoers, these women would have been a highly visible presence in the playhouses. Contemporary documents contain many references to women who served as gatherers. One of them, Elizabeth Wheaton, held that position at both Blackfriars and the Globe.[20] Gatherers were sometimes employed on stage in crowd scenes (Bentley, p. 100), but the existing records do not show whether any of the women who served as gatherers ever appeared in these scenes. Probably they did not: it seems to have been a point of pride with the English professional companies that none of their players were women.

The reason why the English professional companies excluded women from the stage has never been satisfactorily explained, but one of the reasons may have been the players' interest in improving their status. The business of playing was new in late sixteenth-century London, and it was often condemned as a dangerous innovation. The players clearly knew that their exclusion of women was anomalous, and they seem to have exploited that anomaly in an effort to establish their business on a respectable footing. Excluding women from their companies may have been an attempt to insulate themselves both from the taints of effeminacy and immorality that were associated with theatrical impersonation and from the low social status of travelling players. The exclusion of women made the new professional companies look more like the male students who performed Latin plays at Oxford and Cambridge and less like the amateurs who performed in village festivals or the wandering professionals who had travelled across the countryside from time immemorial, both of which included women as well as men. It also provided a basis for claiming superiority to the European professional companies that did include women.

Some of these motives can be seen in Thomas Nashe's defence of playgoing in his *Pierce Penilesse his Supplication to the Divell* (1592), where he emphasized the masculine purity of the English companies as a basis for both national and professional pride. 'Our players', he boasted, 'are not as the players beyond [the] sea, a sort of squirting bawdy comedians, that have whores and common courtesans to play women's parts'. London performances by French and Italian women were condemned by moralists throughout the period. Thomas Norton's 1574 'exhortation' to the Lord Mayor, for instance, complained about 'assemblies to the unchaste, shameless and unnatural tumbling of the Italian women'. Fifty-five years later, Thomas Brande was similarly contemptuous of 'certain vagrant French players': '*those women*', he wrote, 'did attempt, thereby giving just offence to all virtuous and well-disposed persons in this town, to act a certain lascivious and unchaste comedy, in the French tongue at the Blackfriars'.

Despite these condemnations, the foreign actresses were clearly popular. No less an authority than the infamous moralist William

Prynne, for instance, attested to the English popularity of the French company condemned by Brande. Prynne complained in his *Histrio-mastix* that 'there was great resort' to see the '*French-women Actors*, in a Play not long since personated in *Blackfriars Playhouse*', and the same company also performed at two other playhouses, the Red Bull and the Fortune (Orgel, p. 7). The professional success of the foreign companies must have been known to the English players, and they seem to have provided models for emulation. Many of Shakespeare's plays use characters, plot devices, and stage business that have prototypes in the repertory of the Italian *commedia dell'arte*, and Shakespeare had many ways of knowing about these companies and their performances, whether from their English tours, from his fellow actor Will Kempe's visit to Italy, or from the visits by Italian musicians at Queen Elizabeth's court. Confronted with the professional success of the foreign actresses, the English players tried to have it both ways: they showed their own superiority by excluding women from their companies, but they also emulated the most striking attractions of the foreign players, not the least of which was the roles they assigned to women.

Leading women had prominent roles in the Italian companies, not only in performing, but also in scripting the roles they performed. Isabella Andreini, a leading actor, was also famous as a published playwright and poet, but even when they did not produce written scripts, all the actors in the *commedia*—the women as well as the men—were in some measure the authors of their own theatrical selves because they worked from scenarios which required that the actors had to be proficient at onstage improvisation. Shakespeare may have been thinking of these Italian women when he depicted witty, independent heroines such as Rosalind and Portia scripting roles for their own performance.

Medieval and Renaissance English women also wrote the scripts for many plays ranging from liturgical drama to aristocratic and royal entertainments. The names of a number of these women survive, along with the plays they produced: Katherine of Sutton, the four-teenth-century abbess of Barking; the sixteenth-century Countess of Pembroke, whose *Antonie*, published in 1592, influenced the vogue of neo-Senecan drama in England; Elizabeth Cary, who wrote *Mariam the Fair Queen of Jewry*.[21] As far as we know, no women wrote playscripts for the London professional stage during Shakespeare's life-time, but we do know that, as Virginia Woolf shrewdly guessed, many texts that have come down to us as the work of 'Anon' were actually written by women.[22] Woolf's observation is especially pertinent to the case of sixteenth-century playscripts for the public theatres, both because a large proportion of them have come down to us as anonymous and because collaborative authorship was the norm rather than the exception. During the 1580s and 1590s, in fact, about half of the plays produced were anonymous, and although authorial attribution increased during the seventeenth century, a great many plays continued to be registered and produced anonymously throughout Shakespeare's lifetime. Given the fact that the emerging culture of authorship and publication in Shakespeare's England specifically discouraged women from publishing their writing, it would not be surprising to discover that some of these many anonymous plays—as well as some of the plays sold to the players as the work of the men whose names are now associated with them—may actually have been written in whole or in part by women. Female authorship is unlikely to have recommended any publication in Shakespeare's England, and plays were published, just as they were performed, with an eye to profit. Early in Shakespeare's career, title pages on published plays typically listed the name of the playing company that had performed the play, but not the name of the writer. Later, when playwriting had become more respectable and Shakespeare's name had itself become a selling point, even plays he did not write were published as his. Moreover, the very rhetoric of authorship, with its use of terms like 'father' and 'begetter', militated against the acknowledgement of a woman's authority even over the writing she actually produced. The case of Christine de Pizan is instructive. Christine (*c*.1364–1431) was a remarkably prolific author. She wrote on a great variety of subjects, including, but not limited to, arms and chivalry, moral proverbs, courtly entertainments, and defences of women. In fifteenth- and early sixteenth-century England, her books, both in their original French and in English translations, were the most widely read of any female author's. Significantly, however, almost all of the English translations, unlike the French originals, attributed the authorship of Christine's books to men.[23] Christine's prominence, her repeated textual emphasis upon her gender and authorship, and the survival of many early copies of her works have restored her entitlement. In the case of women's authorship of commercial playscripts, however, as in all too much of women's history, although the silences in the existing records are suggestive, the actual facts may never be recovered.

What the records do show is that the offstage presence of women would have exerted a powerful influence upon playscripts even if, as the records seem to indicate, all of them were actually written by men. The most obvious evidence of women's influence is the fact that a number of the London companies had female patrons. The leading company in the 1580s was the Queen's Men, under the patronage of Queen Elizabeth. During the reigns of the Stuarts, Queen Anne, Lady Elizabeth, and Queen Henrietta all issued patents to the companies that took their names (Cerasano and Wynne-Davies, pp. 158–9).[24] Moreover, since the players derived the bulk of their income from public performances, all of the companies, whether or not their official patrons were women, would have been influenced by the fact that women constituted a sizeable proportion of the paying customers in the public playhouses, perhaps more than half. Here too, it is necessary to read between the lines of the existing records. When Andrew Gurr compiled a list of 'every person who can be identified as having seen a play in a commercial playhouse between 1567 and 1642', he found the names of only twenty women. However, as Gurr points out, the records he found are really inadequate for statistical purposes, since 'on a conservative estimate', there were probably fifty million visits to the playhouses during the years in question; and the names of women, like the names of ordinary citizens of both sexes, were less likely to appear in the records than those of gentlemen.[25] Nonetheless, women constituted a visible presence all over the city of London, where they could be seen buying and selling in the markets, assisting in household businesses, running businesses of their own, engaging in litigation on their own account, and in the audiences at the playhouses. In Southwark, the immediate neighbourhood of the theatres, at least sixteen per cent of the households were headed by women, and the prologues and epilogues to many plays explicitly mark the players' awareness that they needed to please female playgoers.

The Epilogue to *As You Like It* is a good case in point. Spoken by the actor who played Rosalind, it addresses female and male playgoers separately, beginning with the women, whom it charges 'to like as much of this play as please you', thus suggesting that the 'you' in the play's title refers primarily to them. Women suffered from numerous disabilities in Shakespeare's England, but the collective economic power they possessed as paying customers in the playhouse meant that none of Shakespeare's plays could have been successful in his own time if it failed to please them. Given the incompleteness and indeterminacy of the historical record, the playscripts themselves may constitute some of the best evidence we have about the desires and interests that women brought with them when they went to the playhouse in Shakespeare's England.

3

Our Canon, Ourselves

Despite the evidence that Shakespeare's plays were initially designed for the pleasure of women as well as men, modern scholars have often identified them as a site of women's repression—evidence of women's subordinate place in his own world and an influential means of validating that subordination for future generations. Women's roles in Shakespeare's plays are far more limited than men's, both in size and in number, and female power is repeatedly characterized as threatening or even demonic. In fact, Shakespeare's representations of women often seem less sympathetic than those of other playwrights working at the same time. The figure of the witch, for instance, memorably demonized in *Macbeth*, appears as an amiable charlatan in Thomas Heywood's *The Wise Woman of Hogsdon*. The title character in Heywood's comedy, although denounced as a witch by dissolute young gallants, turns out to be the agent for effecting their reform and bringing about the desired resolution of the plot. In Rowley, Dekker, and Ford's *The Witch of Edmonton*, the witch is a tragic figure, driven to witchcraft by need and persecution and explicitly stated to be far less guilty than the respectable gentleman who occupies the highest social rank of all the characters in the play.

These are only two of many possible examples. It is interesting, for instance, to compare Shakespeare's treatment of warlike women in his early history plays with their far more sympathetic treatment in the anonymous contemporary play *Edward III*. This play is sometimes attributed to Shakespeare, and it even appears in recent editions of his collected works, but it has yet to achieve a secure place in the Shakespearian canon, and its female characters are depicted in strikingly different terms from those in the canonical Shakespearian history plays. In Shakespeare's *Henry VI, Part 1*, Joan is both the chief enemy to the English kingdom and a witch as well. In *Parts 2* and *3*, Margaret is a bloodthirsty adulteress. The more sympathetically depicted female characters in Shakespeare's history plays, such as the victimized women in *Richard III* and the Duchess of Gloucester and the Queen in *Richard II*, never go to war, they play no part in the affairs of state, and they seem to spend most of their limited time on stage in tears. Helplessness seems to be an essential component of female virtue in most of Shakespeare's English histories. *Edward III*, by contrast, depicts courageous women warriors who are also models of feminine virtue. The Countess of Salisbury resists the Scots king's siege of her castle and the English king's assault on her virtue with equal courage and resolution. The English queen, equally virtuous, leads her army to victory over the Scots at Newcastle, 'big with child' but still 'every day in arms' (IV.ii.40–6).[1] In *Edward III*, warlike English women defend their country against foreign threats. In Shakespeare's English history plays, warlike women *embody* those threats. Both Joan's French nationality and Margaret's are repeatedly emphasized, and both are depicted as threatening to the well-being and stability of the English kingdom. Similarly, in *Henry IV, Part 1*, in which the foreign enemies are Welsh, the opening scene describes the Welsh women's mutilation of the corpses of the English soldiers killed in battle against Owen Glyndŵr. No women fight on the side of the English.

Comparisons between Shakespeare's representations of women and those of his fellow playwrights suggest that a too-exclusive focus on Shakespeare may produce a misleading picture of the assumptions about women's roles that early modern English playgoers were prepared to accept. But even within the Shakespearian canon, there are indications of a more generous view of women's place than the examples typically cited in recent scholarship have seemed to suggest. In fact, the plays that modern scholars have chosen to emphasize may tell us more about our own assumptions regarding women than about the beliefs that informed the responses of Shakespeare's first audiences. Among the history plays, for example, the one that is most frequently taught and probably most admired is *Henry IV, Part 1*. This is also the one in which female characters are most marginalized, speaking less than 3.5 per cent of the words in the script. Female characters are much more prominent in the *Henry VI* plays, *King John*, and *Henry VIII*. In Shakespeare's better-known history plays, women's roles are severely limited, both in size and in scope. The places where history is made—the royal court, the council-chamber, and the field of battle—are overwhelmingly male preserves, and the business of the main historical plots is conducted entirely by men. However, the picture changes if we look at the other plays I have named. All three parts of *Henry VI*, as well as *King John*, feature women in what are now considered 'untraditional' roles—as generals leading victorious armies on the battlefield and as political actors who exercise significant power in the conduct of state affairs. Unlike Shakespeare's better-known history plays, these plays feature active, energetic female characters. Their roles may be unsympathetic, but they are real players in the theatre of history. These plays are much less frequently performed or taught. In fact, there is an almost perfect inverse correlation between the prominence of women's roles in a history play and the play's current reputation. In the most highly esteemed of Shakespeare's history plays—*Richard II*, the two parts of *Henry IV*, and *Henry V*—the percentage of words assigned to female characters never reaches 10 per cent of the script, and the women who do appear are typically confined, either to enclosed domestic settings or to the fictional lowlife world of Mistress Quickly's tavern in Eastcheap. Often designated by modern scholars as 'The Henriad', these plays are the ones most admired by scholars and critics, and they are also most frequently produced on stage and best known by the general public.

The responses of Shakespeare's earliest audiences may have been strikingly different.[2] In the case of *Henry VI, Part 1*, for instance, Thomas Nashe wrote in 1592 that 'ten thousand spectators (at least)' had seen that play, and Philip Henslowe's records of the receipts for its initial run suggest a figure closer to twenty thousand, more than all but one of the many other plays that Henslowe produced. It may very well be that we, much more than Shakespeare's original audience, prefer the plays that minimize the roles of women and depict female characters in stereotypically 'feminine' roles and settings. If that is the case, our negative estimation of these early plays—and also of women's place in Shakespeare's English histories—may tell us more about our own limitations than about those of Shakespeare and his original audiences.

A similar argument can be made for whatever genre of Shakespearian plays we choose to compare. The patriarchal fantasy played out in *The Tempest* has proved much more attractive to modern scholars and theatre audiences than any of the other late romances, all of which include more, and more powerful, roles for female characters. Our paradigmatic Shakespearian tragedy is *Hamlet*; it is interesting to contemplate the ways our picture of women's place in Shakespeare's plays would be altered if it were *Antony and Cleopatra*. Probably the best illustration of this effect, however, can be found in the comedies, because comedy was the genre that focused most frequently on women, sex, and gender.

Two comedies that illustrate with remarkable clarity the modern preference for stories in which women are put in their (subordinate) place are *The Taming of the Shrew* and *The Merry Wives of Windsor*. *The Taming of the Shrew* has enjoyed exceptional popularity in recent years, while *The Merry Wives of Windsor*, which offers a much more benign view of women's place in marriage (and also seems to have been modelled much more closely on the world that Shakespeare and his audiences actually knew), has been relatively neglected. During the years between 1979 and 1993, for instance, the Royal Shakespeare Company staged *The Taming of the Shrew* twice as often as *The Merry Wives of Windsor* (twelve times as opposed to six).[3] *The Taming of the Shrew* has also been favoured by scholars. As I mentioned in Chapter 1, *The MLA International Bibliography of Books and Articles on the Modern Language and Literatures* shows that *The Taming of the Shrew* has attracted far more critical and scholarly attention than any other of Shakespeare's early comedies. *The Shrew* has been equally popular with the general public. One of the most frequently produced of all Shakespeare's plays, it also became, in 1929, the first to be presented in a talking film. Since then, it has provided the basis for innumerable other films, stage productions, and spinoffs. The hit musical *Kiss Me Kate* is the best known, but there have been many others.

There is no evidence that the play enjoyed a comparable popularity when it was first performed. Although it is usually dated in the early 1590s, it does not appear among the titles cited in 1598 in Francis

Meres's *Palladis Tamia* as examples of Shakespeare's excellence as a playwright. Meres lists five early comedies—*The Two Gentlemen of Verona*, *The Comedy of Errors*, *Love's Labour's Lost*, *A Midsummer Night's Dream*, and *The Merchant of Venice*. Unless *The Taming of the Shrew* is the unidentified play Meres called 'Love's Labour's Won', it was not included in his list, even though it is generally believed to have appeared during or before the 1593–4 theatrical season. Another indication that the play may not have been much admired—or even noticed—in Shakespeare's time is the fact that there are only three recorded references to it before 1649.[4] The performance history is equally skimpy: only three were recorded before the end of the seventeenth century. The first of these performances dates from 1633, when it was followed two days later by *The Woman's Prize, or The Tamer Tamed*, a sequel written around 1611 by John Fletcher, Shakespeare's successor as the leading playwright for the King's Men. In Fletcher's play, the tables are turned, and Petruchio gets his comeuppance. Ann Thompson notes that this was the only case in which one of Shakespeare's plays 'provoked a theatrical "reply" ' during his own lifetime.[5]

In *The Tamer Tamed*, Petruchio, now widowed, marries a spirited young woman named Maria who resolves to tame the notorious shrew-tamer. Although Maria admits that she freely chose Petruchio for her husband and would choose him again 'before the best man living' (1.3.155), she locks and barricades the house against him and refuses to let him enter or consummate the marriage until he has been properly tamed. Clearly designed as a response to Shakespeare's play, *The Tamer Tamed* opens with a scene in which three men debate Petruchio's merits as a husband. Two of them—Tranio, who bears the name of the sympathetic character from the earlier play, and Sophocles, whose name suggests wisdom—condemn his rough, domineering ways. His only defender is Moroso, who places the blame on Kate; but Moroso is clearly identified as an unsympathetic character—an old man who wants to marry the romantic heroine Livia, who is herself in love with Rowland. The scene ends with both of the other men expressing their hopes that Moroso will never marry Livia. The Livia/Rowland/Moroso subplot also offers an implicit rebuttal to the earlier play, with its auction for Bianca's hand and the monetary bargaining over Katherine's marriage to Petruchio. The undesirable match between Moroso and Livia is based on mercenary motives and paternal choice, while the desirable marriage between Livia and Rowland is based on Livia's own free choice. In the second scene of the play, Livia assures her lover, 'no man shall make use of me; | My beauty was born free, and free I'll give it | To him that loves, not buys me' (1.2.37–9). Throughout *The Tamer Tamed*, love is repeatedly opposed to mercenary considerations: Maria proclaims that she'd take Petruchio 'In's shirt, with one ten Groats to pay the Priest, | Before the best man living' (II.iii.154–5), and Petruchio declares that he married Maria for her wit (IV.ii.26)—a statement that offers a direct contrast to Shakespeare's Petruccio's declaration that he will marry any woman who is 'rich enough to be Petruccio's wife', regardless of her age, appearance, or temperament (1.2.63–73). At the end of Fletcher's play, Rowland is overjoyed to learn he will lose the money he has bet Tranio because it means he will have Livia (V.iii.36). At the end of Shakespeare's play, by contrast, Petruccio wins both his bet and an increased dowry. At the court of Charles I, where Fletcher's play was presented along with Shakespeare's, *The Taming of the Shrew* was 'liked', but *The Tamer Tamed* was 'very well liked'.[6]

Despite the lack of evidence that *The Taming of the Shrew* was well received in its own time, recent scholarship has often proceeded on the assumption that the story it tells exemplifies beliefs that governed the attitudes of Shakespeare and his contemporaries regarding women's place in marriage. It may very well be, however, that our preoccupation with this crudely misogynist story tells us more about our own biases than about those of Shakespeare's original audience. The same anxieties that made Laura Doyle's guidebook for women, *The Surrendered Wife: A Practical Guide to Finding Intimacy, Passion, and Peace with Your Man* a best-seller in the year 2001 seem to have made Kate's taming a deeply satisfying fantasy to audiences ranging from Harold Bloom to the many filmgoers who paid to see the more than eighteen films that have made *Shrew* one of the most popular of all Shakespeare's plays for production on the modern screen. Women have also bought into the fantasy. They are, after all, the primary audience for *The Surrendered Wife*. Deirdre Donahue wrote in *USA Today* that the book's author, 'a self-described "former shrew," offers a surprisingly honest recipe for getting along with the man you married'. Bloom describes his admiration for *The Taming of the Shrew* in

strikingly similar terms: 'One would have to be tone deaf (or ideologically crazed) not to hear in this [the dialogue between Kate and
Petruccio at 5.1.122–31] a subtly exquisite music of marriage at its
happiest.'[7] Meryl Streep, who played the part of Katherine for Joseph
Papp, seems to have heard the same music: 'Really what matters', she
has said, 'is that they have an incredible passion and love; it's not
something that Katherine admits to right away but it does provide the
source of her change.'[8]

Seen in the context of current anxieties, desires, and beliefs,
Shakespeare's play seems to prefigure the most oppressive modern
assumptions about women and to validate those assumptions as
timeless truths, already present in a sixteenth-century text and already
apparent to Shakespeare's original audiences. However, the play
would have looked very different when it was first performed. One
telling indication of that difference is the fact that modern productions of *The Taming of the Shrew* often cut or rewrite the Induction,
which frames the action as a play within a play. Katherine's final
speech of submission relies heavily on the fiction of a woman's body
beneath her costume, arguing, as it does, that women's subjugation to
men is required by their embodied weakness:

> Why are our bodies soft, and weak, and smooth,
> Unapt to toil and trouble in the world,
> But that our soft conditions and our hearts
> Should well agree with our external parts?
>
> (5.2.169–72)

This speech, which naturalizes women's subordination, works well in
a modern production, in which the actor who plays Kate really is a
woman. The ideological work it accomplishes is less assured if it is
performed (as it often is not, especially in film versions) with the old
Induction framing the action. For there, in the page's cross-dressed
disguise as Christopher Sly's wife, feminine submission is staged as a
theatrical show designed and performed by men in order to trick a
drunken tinker with delusions of grandeur.

Sly is 'Wrapped in sweet clothes', with rings on his fingers, a 'most
delicious banquet by his bed, | And brave attendants near him when he
wakes', but he is still not convinced that he really is a nobleman who

has lost his memory until he is told that he has a beautiful lady who has been weeping about his affliction. The page Bartholomew, disguised in a lady's clothes and weeping with the help of an onion concealed in a napkin, is needed to complete the illusion. 'My husband and my lord, my lord and husband', Bartholomew says: 'I am your wife in all obedience' (Induction 2.203–4). Bartholomew's act parodically foreshadows Kate's declarations of submission to Petruccio at the end of the play. Whether or not the same actor played the parts of Bartholomew and Kate, the page's performance of femininity in the Induction implicitly destabilizes the performance of femininity by the boy actor who played Kate's part in the taming plot.

Spoken by a woman actor, the implications of Kate's final speech are radically transformed. As George Bernard Shaw noted at the end of the nineteenth century,

No man with any decency of feeling can sit it out in the company of a woman without being extremely ashamed of the lord-of-creation moral implied in the wager and the speech put into the woman's own mouth. (quoted in Thompson, p. 21)

Presented by a cross-dressed boy, however, Katherine's proclamation can be seen as a male performance of female compliance, especially if the play is performed with the Induction in which the cross-dressed page persuades a drunken tinker that he is truly a lord by obsequiously performing the role of his obedient wife. Thus, although the marriage plot affirms the authority of patriarchy, the repressive implications of the action it represents are undermined by the initial reminder to the audience that what they are watching is a performance of theatrical shape-shifting. This effect would be intensified if the play were performed—as it probably was—as farce, for the action is replete with slapstick comedy, and the characters are portrayed in one-dimensional stereotypes.

Framed by the Induction, the taming plot comes to the audience as a farcical theatrical performance rather than a representation of actual life. Similar farcical stories would have been familiar to Shakespeare's original audience from widely circulated folk tales and ballads. This version, explicitly set in Italy, might also have recalled the fantastic travellers' tales that were popular at the time the play was written, for the taming plot begins with the arrival of two travellers—Lucentio,

who has come to Padua from Florence; and Petruccio, who has come
from Verona. The only part of the play that is set in a recognizable
contemporary England is the Induction; and the only female character who appears there is the Hostess, who ejects Sly from her tavern
and threatens to fetch the constable to punish him.

As short as it is, the Induction is studded with specific details that
set the action in the here-and-now of the world that Shakespeare and
his audience actually inhabited. Sly identifies the home of his father
as 'Burton-heath'; Barton-on-the Heath was a village about sixteen
miles south of Stratford, where Shakespeare's aunt lived. The Hostess
who threatens Sly in the opening lines of the Induction is 'Marian
Hacket, the fat ale-wife of Wincot'; there was, in the sixteenth
century, a Hacket family living in Wincot, a hamlet about four
miles south of Stratford. These specific references may have provided
in-jokes for Shakespeare's fellow actors and for the members of the
audience who knew the countryside around Stratford; but even for
those who did not catch the specific allusions, the setting of the
Induction would have recalled the familiar features of English village
life, where the trade of ale-wife traditionally belonged to women and
drunken tinkers were a far more familiar sight than Italian gentlemen.
In the taming plot none of the women have any trade at all or any
means of economic support that is not provided by their fathers or
husbands. Given what we know about the widespread economic
activity of women in sixteenth-century England, the roles of women
in the taming plot look much more like a wistful fantasy than a
recognizable representation of the kind of women that Shakespeare
and his first audiences would have been likely to encounter in their
daily lives.

Recent scholars have often interpreted this fantasy as a response to
the anxious desires of Shakespeare's countrymen, confronted by various manifestations of female power, ranging from the monarchy of
Queen Elizabeth at the top of the social hierarchy to the railings of
village scolds and the riots of unruly women at its lower reaches
protesting the rising prices of food. Certainly, the shrew-taming
story has served a similar function for modern admirers of the play
who are manifestly unhappy with the growing assertiveness of women
in their own world. However, it is probably a mistake to read the place
of that fantasy in the cultural imagination of Shakespeare's contem-

poraries as if it were identical to its impact in a world where women's power and assertiveness are visibly increasing. The prominence of women in the twenty-first-century academy, for instance, is a new phenomenon; in Shakespeare's England, what was new were the increased calls for the domestication of women and women's increasing exclusion from many trades in which they had formerly been active. Moreover, there is no evidence that the taming plot attracted as much attention in Shakespeare's time as it has done in our own. A mid-sixteenth-century English ballad, 'A Merry Jest of a Shrewd and Curst Wife Lapped in Morel's Skin for Her Good Behaviour', is often cited by modern scholars both as a possible source for Shakespeare's taming plot and as evidence that such stories were extremely popular in the period, but it is important to note both that the ballad was printed only once[9] and that early allusions to Shakespeare's play tend to focus not on the taming plot but on the frame story, where the butt of the joke is not an unruly woman but an unruly poor man.

The trick the Lord plays on Sly depends for its shock value on the pretence that the poor tinker is a nobleman: what is in question are not the distinctions that separate men from women but those that separate people who occupy disparate ranks in the social hierarchy. Those distinctions, which were a matter of persistent and compelling interest in Shakespeare's world, surface again in the taming plot when the clever servant Tranio impersonates his master; but in the Induction, they are the only distinctions that seem to matter. At the end of the first scene of the Induction, for instance, the Lord declares,

> I know the boy will well usurp the grace,
> Voice, gait, and action of a gentlewoman.
> I long to hear him call the drunkard husband,
> And how my men will stay themselves from laughter
> When they do homage to this simple peasant.

What threatens to provoke uncontrollable laughter in the participants is not the boy's disguise as a gentlewoman but the pretence that a simple peasant is a nobleman. Since this is also the point of the entire charade, it was presumably also what was designed to titillate and amuse the playgoers.

And amuse them it did. There is considerable evidence that early audiences favoured the Sly plot. A version of the play called *The Taming of a Shrew* in which Sly reappeared at various points of the play and at the end as well to offer his comments upon the action was printed in various Quarto editions, the first of which, published in 1594, stated on its title page that the play had been 'sundry times acted'. It is also noteworthy that this play was less stridently male-supremacist than the version that appeared in the First Folio edition of Shakespeare's plays (Marcus, pp. 177–200). The fact that *The Taming of the Shrew* did not appear in print until the First Folio suggests that it may have been less popular than the other version, since Quarto editions may have been produced to capitalize upon a demand for printed copies of plays that had been popular in perform-ance.[10] In any event, it was Sly's story, not the taming plot, that featured in several early recorded comments on the play. John Dryden, in fact, compared Sly to Shakespeare himself, when he wrote in 1672, 'Thus like the drunken Tinker in his play, | He grew a Prince, and never knew which way' (*Allusion-Book* II, p. 172). The Induction material was also expanded to form the basis of two eighteenth-century plays, both called *The Cobbler of Preston*. One of these was so popular that it was reprinted in eight editions.

This is not to say that the taming plot was forgotten. It formed the basis of David Garrick's popular three-act farce, *Catharine and Pet-ruchio*, which was virtually the only version staged from the time it was written in 1754 until the middle of the following century.[11] In fact, of all Shakespeare's plays, *The Taming of the Shrew* was the last to be restored to its original form on stage (Thompson, p. 20). It is easy to see why eighteenth- and nineteenth-century playgoers found Gar-rick's version of the taming plot more palatable than its Shakespear-ian prototype. In Garrick's final scene, when Baptista offers to give Petruchio an additional dowry for his newly reformed daughter, Petruchio, now as indifferent to mercenary advantage as the faithful lovers in Fletcher's play, immediately refuses, declaring:

> My Fortune is sufficient. Here's my Wealth:
> Kiss me, my *Kate*; and since thou art become
> So prudent, kind, and dutiful a Wife,
> *Petruchio* here shall doff the lordly Husband;

An honest Mask, which I throw off with Pleasure.
Far hence all Rudeness, Wilfulness, and Noise,
And be our future Lives one gentle Stream
Of mutual Love, Compliance and Regard.[12]

Garrick's revisions of the play are revealing not only because they display the impact of a changing gender ideology but also because they anticipate the celebratory modern readings that have made the play so popular in our own time. Not only our preferences among the Shakespearian canon but also our interpretations of the plays we prefer are clearly shaped by the pressures of our own time and place. Garrick's Petruchio prefigures the recurrent plot motif identified by Janice Radway in twentieth-century popular romance novels when he makes it clear at the end of the play (as Shakespeare's Petruccio does not) that his loveless behaviour was a mere screen for his true feelings, easily thrown aside once his wife has learned to be dutifully obedient. This is not to say that he promises an equal relationship. Garrick makes sure that it is Petruchio rather than Catharine who has the last word, and in his very next speech—the final speech in the play—he recites the lines Shakespeare had given his Katherine to authorize wifely subordination by analogy to the subordination of subjects to monarchs.

Like Garrick's play, the romances Radway studied end in the promise of a happy, loving marriage, when, despite the apparent cruelty of their hyper-masculine, aggressive heroes, it turns out that they really care for the heroines. The heroines, in turn, abandon their own defiant and inappropriately masculine behaviour because, 'Like all romances, these novels eventually recommend the usual sexual division of labor that dictates that women take charge of the domestic and purely personal spheres of human endeavor.'[13] Many other features of Garrick's play—and of Shakespeare's as well—also prefigure those novels, and Radway's analysis of the cultural work the novels perform helps to explain the widespread appeal Shakespeare's play has acquired in recent years—years when one out of every six mass-market paperbacks sold in North America is a Harlequin or Silhouette romance novel.[14] Katherine, like the heroines preferred by the late twentieth-century women readers Radway surveyed, 'is differentiated ... by an extraordinarily fiery disposition' and 'the particularly exaggerated quality of her early rebelliousness against parental strictures'. Like them, Katherine also 'explicitly refuse[s] to be silenced by the male desire to control women through the eradication of their individual voices'. '[S]peak I will', she insists:

> My tongue will tell the anger of my heart,
> Or else my heart concealing it will break,
> And rather than it shall, I will be free,
> Even to the uttermost, as I please, in words.
>
> (4.3.74–80)

Even the fact that most of Katherine's ordeal takes place at Petruccio's house in the country has a counterpart in the modern romances Radway studied, in which the heroine is typically removed from the familiar realm associated with her childhood and family (pp. 123–4). These novels, in Radway's analysis, express and assuage their readers' ambivalences about the constraints that define their roles as women in our own culture. Specifically, the novels place the blame for men's 'rigid indifference and their mistreatment of women', not on the men's own 'indifference, competitiveness, or ambition', but instead on the 'women's own insufficiency as perfect wife-mothers' (p. 128). Only after the heroine has learned to behave like a true woman will the hero be transformed into an ideal figure who, while retaining his masculine power, will also be able to care for her in a tender, solicitous way that satisfies the readers' desires (pp. 127–8).

This is not to say that all of the features preferred by the romance readers Radway studied are present in *The Taming of the Shrew*. Significantly, a crucial characteristic of the modern romance hero is the fact that 'the terrorizing effect of his exemplary masculinity is always tempered by the presence of a small feature that introduces an important element of softness into the overall picture' (p. 128). No such feature appears in Shakespeare's characterization of Petruccio, but it is revealing that modern readers of the play have been at great pains to discover it. According to an early twentieth-century editor, for instance,

there is a delicacy in the man underlying his boisterousness throughout. . . . He has to tame this termagant bride of his, and he does it in action with a very harsh severity. But while he storms and raves among servants and tailors, showing off for her benefit, to her his speech remains courteous and restrained—well restrained and, with its ironical excess, elaborately courteous. It is observable, that, through all the trials he imposes on her, he never says the sort of misprising word that hurts a high-mettled woman more than any rough deed.[15]

Quiller-Couch is clearly an apologist for Petruccio and for the taming plot. Like a number of recent critics, he waxes sentimental about the play's conclusion, declaring that 'there are truly few prettier conclusions in Shakespeare than [Katherine's] final submission' (p. 43); but because he is less guarded than they are in expressing the reasons for his admiration, his remarks are worth quoting in some detail:

it is not discreet perhaps for an editor to discuss, save historically, the effective ways of dealing with [shrews]. Petruchio's was undoubtedly drastic and has gone out of fashion. But avoiding the present times and recalling ... Dickens's long gallery of middle-aged wives who make household life intolerable by various and odious methods, one cannot help thinking a little wistfully that the Petruchian discipline had something to say for itself. It may be that these curses on the hearth are an inheritance of our middle-class, exacerbating wives by deserting them, most of the day, for desks and professional routine; that the high feudal lord would have none of it, and as little would the rough serf or labourer with an unrestrained hand. Let it suffice to say that *The Taming of the Shrew* belongs to a period, and is not ungallant, even so. The works of our author do not enforce set lessons in morals. . . . He is nowhere an expositor of creed or dogma, but simply always an exhorter, by quiet catholic influence, to valiancy and noble conduct of life. (pp. xxvi–vii)

Clearly, this early twentieth-century editor's response to the play is fuelled by his own longing for a world in which wives can be tamed by whatever means it takes. Apparently embarrassed by his self-revelation, however, he immediately retreats into historicism, disavowing his very personal and contemporary response by 'avoiding the present times' and reminding his readers that '*The Taming of the Shrew* belongs to a period'. Quiller-Couch's essay is itself a period piece, and the period to which it belongs is his own. His reading of the play tells us much more about the donnish early-twentieth-century social milieu in which he wrote than it does about the world in which the play was originally produced. Both the nakedness of his self-revelation and the historical veil with which he quickly attempts to conceal it prefigure in the simplest possible terms and with amazing clarity the social and psychological mechanisms that went into the construction of the twentieth-century image of a patriarchal bard.[16] For readers like Quiller-Couch, that image has been the object of wistful desire; for feminist critics it has produced a set of texts so inimical to feminist reading that 'feminist criticism . . . is restricted to exposing its own exclusion' (McLuskie, p. 97).

Quiller-Couch and many of his successors have attempted to whitewash the oppressiveness of Katherine's taming. More recently, feminist scholars, such as Lynda Boose and Frances Dolan, have refuted their arguments by exposing both the brutality of the represented action and its dreadful historical implications. The stakes in these critical debates have been high, but one unfortunate consequence of the interest they have attracted is that despite the lack of evidence that the play was popular in its own time, it has taken on, not only in the popular imagination but also in feminist scholarship, the status of the paradigmatic Shakespearian representation of women's place in marriage.[17]

The Merry Wives of Windsor

The play that probably should occupy that status is *The Merry Wives of Windsor*, both because of the unequalled prominence of married women and marital relationships in the action and because it is the only Shakespearian comedy set in a recognizable, contemporary England. With its location in an actual town situated not far from London, its characters taken from the middle ranks of society, and its representation of the homely details of everyday life, it comes closest in characterization and setting to the actual world that Shakespeare and his original audiences inhabited. The script is laced with references to specific locations in and around Windsor, such as Frogmore, a nearby village (2.3.65) and Datchet Mead (3.3.11), a meadow situated between Windsor Little Park and the Thames.[18] Instead of romantic adventures in far-off places, the audience hears about the familiar activities of everyday life. There are whitsters (that is, linen bleachers) in Datchet Mead; Mistress Ford has a buck-basket for her laundry and a cowl-staff for her servants to carry it; Mistress Quickly complains that she has to 'wash, wring, brew, bake, scour, dress meat and drink, [and] make the beds' (1.4.84–5). Here, unlike *Macbeth*, perfumes are identified not as coming from Arabia but as having been purchased in Bucklesbury, a London street where herbs were sold (3.3.61). Here, unlike *A Midsummer Night's Dream*, the fairies who appear in the woods outside the town are town children in masquerade.

In this recognizably contemporary English town, women are gainfully employed, run households, supervise servants, and arrange marriages. The only husband who attempts to exercise the kind of patriarchal surveillance that recent critics have assumed as the historical norm is Ford; but instead of being taken seriously, Ford's anxiety about his wife's fidelity makes him the object of his neighbours' ridicule. To at least one seventeenth-century Englishwoman, the roles and representations of women in *The Merry Wives of Windsor* rang remarkably true. Margaret Cavendish, the author of the first critical essay ever published on Shakespeare, regarded Shakespeare's representations of female characters as one of his greatest strengths. Among the eight characters she cited as examples, four are from *The Merry Wives of Windsor*. '[O]ne would think', she wrote,

he had been Metamorphosed from a Man to a Woman, for who could Describe *Cleopatra* Better than he hath done, and many other Females of his own Creating, as *Nan Page*, *Mrs. Page*, *Mrs. Ford*, the Doctors Maid, *Bettrice*, Mrs. *Quickly*, *Doll Tearsheet*, and others, too many to Relate?[19]

In the vastly different England of the turn of the twentieth century, another woman recorded a similar response. In 1902, Rosa Grindon, the President of the Manchester Ladies Literary and Scientific Club, published her monograph 'In Praise of Shakespeare's *Merry Wives of Windsor*: An Essay in Exposition and Appreciation'. Grindon's argument is worth noting because by the time she wrote, *The Merry Wives* was rarely performed and almost universally disparaged as a second- or third-rate play, and her monograph was an attempt to defend the play against the by-then-prevailing judgement that it was vastly inferior to Shakespeare's other works. Grindon explained and answered the criticisms by invoking the tradition that the play had been written at Queen Elizabeth's command. Since the play had been written for a woman, she argued, women were best suited to understand and judge it.[20]

The eighteenth-century tradition that *The Merry Wives* was originally written at the request of Queen Elizabeth has never been verified, but it has had a remarkable persistence, often as an explanation for what seemed to be the play's inferiority as the result both of hasty composition and of Shakespeare's lack of interest in the project. Perhaps, however, there is something to be said for Rosa Grindon's argument—not her assumption that the story about Queen Elizabeth was true, but her sense that it expressed something essential about the curiously negative reputation the play had acquired by the time she wrote. The tradition connecting the play to Queen Elizabeth may very well owe its persistence to the critics' sense that this play was in fact designed to address the interests of women—an intuition that may also help to explain the play's lack of interest and esteem in a scholarly tradition that has been overwhelmingly shaped by men. What is more difficult to explain, however, is the fact that until very recently the play has also been surprisingly absent from most of the twentieth-century feminist scholarship that examined women's place in Shakespeare's plays and its relation to their place in the historical world he inhabited.[21] Following the mainstream of popular and scholarly interest, feminist criticism often focused instead on the extravagant stories in the other comedies, which (perhaps not incidentally) tend to depict women in much less empowered—and much less familiar—roles.

The fact that the history of *The Merry Wives'* reputation can be plotted on a trajectory almost exactly opposite to that of *The Taming of the Shrew* suggests that some of the same cultural forces have been involved. Throughout the twentieth century, as *The Taming of the Shrew* received more and more attention, *The Merry Wives* was dismissed or ignored in virtually every study of Shakespeare's comedies.[22] Both the dismissal of *The Merry Wives* and the current interest in *The Taming of the Shrew* appear to be the products of a distinctively modern taste, because—again in direct contrast to the *Shrew*—*The Merry Wives* was extremely popular throughout most of its earlier history. When the theatres reopened after the Restoration, it was one of the first of Shakespeare's plays to be revived on stage, and was one of the most popular plays in the new repertory. Its supremacy continued well into the eighteenth century. During the years 1701 to 1750, in fact, it was produced over two hundred times, more than any

of Shakespeare's other comedies.[23] Moreover, the play's critical reputation equalled its popularity on stage. John Dryden praised it, both in
his essay *Of Dramatic Poesie* and in his Preface to the revised version
of *Troilus and Cressida*, as the most 'regular' and 'exactly form'd' of all
Shakespeare's compositions (Taylor, p. 30). Charles Gildon wrote in
1702 that it was Shakespeare's only 'true comedy', and Joseph Warton
declared in 1778 that it was 'the most complete specimen of Shakespeare's comic powers'. Samuel Johnson noted that 'its general power,
that power by which all works of genius shall finally be tried, is such,
that perhaps it never yet had reader or spectator, who did not think it
too soon at an end'.[24]

Even in the nineteenth century, when the play's reputation was in
decline, it could still evoke enthusiastic responses from editors. In
1820, William Oxberry wrote, 'this delightful comedy is perfect'; and
Samuel William Singer declared in 1826 that 'the incidents, characters, and plot of this delightful comedy are unrivalled in any drama,
ancient or modern' (Roberts, pp. 62–3). It was also valued for its
representation of sixteenth-century English life, as in this nostalgic
encomium from one late nineteenth-century admirer:

The whirligig of time and death must run its round, ere ever they bring back
Shakespeare's England out of the dust of years. . . . But in the enchanted pages
the old world dwells secure . . . [It lies] in Shakespeare's pages, and you have
but to throw down the . . . newspapers, to open the volume, and your life is
that you would gladlier have lived in the larger, airier, more kindly and
congenial days, 'the spacious days of great Elizabeth'.[25]

To the political theorist Friedrich Engels 'the first act of the *Merry
Wives* alone contains more life and reality than all German literature'.[26] To the Shakespeare scholar Felix Schelling, there was 'no
play of Shakespeare's which draws so unmistakably on his own experience of English life as this, and the dramatist's real source here is
undoubtedly the life of the Elizabethans'.[27]

That very realism, however, probably helped to marginalize the
play in the mainstream of post-Romantic criticism, with its vener-
ation for poetry and imaginative flights of fancy. Instead of encouraging its audiences to imagine a timeless, ideal world, it imitates the
very specific world of late sixteenth-century England. As Frederick
Wedmore wrote in 1874, 'Here then, perhaps more than elsewhere as a

whole has Shakspere...[drawn] from just the common life about' him, but the result is that the play depicts 'usages we do not recognize, types we have forgotten'.[28] A striking anomaly in the canon of Shakespeare's comedies, the play had no place in the universe of marvellous invention and fine poetry they seemed to inhabit. There are brief glimpses of similarly down-to-earth, contemporary settings in other plays, most notably in the Gloucestershire scenes in *Henry IV, Part 2* and the Induction to *The Taming of the Shrew*, both of which depict scenes and characters that are based on the life Shakespeare and many of the members of his audience must have known; but the setting for the typical Shakespearian comedy is a distant or imaginary place, where the leading characters have no visible means of support and no business more serious than falling in and out of love and pursuing the objects of their romantic desire. In *The Merry Wives*, Fenton's courtship of Anne, which would have been the main plot in a standard Shakespearian romantic comedy, is given very little time on stage. The main business of this play is Falstaff's inept, mercenary pursuit of the Windsor wives, which, as Arthur F. Kinney has observed, serves as a parody of the traditional business of romantic comedy.[29] Even the language of *The Merry Wives of Windsor* is peculiar. Written predominantly in prose—more prose, in fact, than in any other Shakespearian playscript—it seems much closer to the language of actual, everyday life. All these anomalies probably contributed to the failure of *The Merry Wives of Windsor* to find a place in twentieth-century studies of Shakespeare's comedies, where it was either ignored or dismissed as distinctly inferior to the others (Roberts, pp. 65–6).

The striking differences between the here-and-now of Shakespeare's familiar, contemporary Windsor and the glamorous, remote worlds his other plays evoked for the imagination often seemed a terrible disappointment to the playwright's romantically minded admirers. The fairies who torment Falstaff are actually town children in masquerade, and their queen is none other than Mistress Quickly. Male sexual insecurity is equally subject to common-sense demystification. Instead of being taken seriously as a motive for tragic action, the irrational jealousy that threatens to kill Hermione and does kill Desdemona does no harm at all to Ford's merry wife: its only consequence is to make him the object of his neighbours' ridicule.

What was most disappointing, however, was the effect of this new environment on Falstaff.

From Maurice Morgann to Harold Bloom, male critics have fallen in love with the Falstaff of the history plays and identified with him. To them, he has been far more than a character in a play: pulsating with vivid life, he seemed to transcend both the historical moment of his creation and the historical world in which Shakespeare originally installed him to take his place in their imaginations as a kindred spirit. In the context of the history plays, the fact that Falstaff was a fictional character gave him a unique place in the historical action. The fact that the predominant language of those plays was blank verse meant that Falstaff's witty, irreverent prose had the effect of spontaneous, unpredictable present speech. His irrepressible, transgressive eloquence enabled him to debunk the conventional pieties that defined the limits of historical representation. He seemed to break through the frame of the represented action to join the audience in an eternal theatrical present. In *The Merry Wives of Windsor*, by contrast, while Falstaff is still an outsider in the world of the play, he no longer enjoys a privileged relationship either with the play's original audience or with its later readers. Here, he speaks the same language and occupies the same frame of representation as the other characters in a setting that recalls the particular here-and-now of the original, late sixteenth-century audience's experience.

In the Henry IV plays, Falstaff could talk his way out of paying for his misdeeds. In the contemporary, physically grounded setting of *The Merry Wives of Windsor*, verbal facility is no longer privileged. Mistress Quickly's speech is still riddled with malapropisms, but while they made her the butt of Falstaff's jokes in the Henry IV plays, in which she was easily victimized by his empty promises of marriage and his unpaid debts, it is now equally easy for her to outwit Falstaff as she repeatedly lures him into the traps set by the wives. And at the end of the play, she supervises his punishments as Falstaff is made to 'stand at the taunt of [another verbally inept character, the Welsh parson] who makes fritters of English' (5.5.135–6). In the history plays, Falstaff's theatrical power is supreme: he even upstages the future king of England. In the familiar, contemporary world of the Windsor wives, he is a beached whale, helplessly gasping on a shore he cannot navigate (2.1.56–7). He is repeatedly humiliated by the town wives, who arrange for him to be buried in dirty laundry, dunked in a muddy stream, convinced to disguise himself as a fat woman, beaten with a cudgel, and tormented by little children, whom he is gullible enough to take for fairies.

To Falstaff's critical admirers, the transformation was intolerable. To William Hazlitt, the Falstaff of *The Merry Wives* 'is like a person recalled to the stage to perform an unaccustomed and ungracious part': he 'is not the man he was in the two parts of *Henry IV* '.[30] To Edward Dowden, Shakespeare 'dressed up a fat rogue, brought forward for the occasion from the back premises of the poet's imagination, in Falstaff's clothes'.[31] In our own time, Harold Bloom echoes the judgements of numerous predecessors when he calls the Falstaff of *The Merry Wives* 'a rank impostor'. In fact, both Hartley Coleridge and A. C. Bradley had used exactly the same term: to Coleridge, he was a 'big-bellied impostor', to Bradley simply 'the impostor'. The play, Bradley thought, showed evidence of hasty composition, and the spectacle of a 'disreputable fat old knight called Falstaff' 'baffled, duped, treated like dirty linen, beaten, burnt, pricked, mocked, insulted, and, worst of all, repentant and didactic' was 'horrible'.[32] Perhaps most 'horrible' was the fact that Falstaff's humiliations are devised by women. Like Fletcher's sequel to *The Taming of the Shrew*, *The Merry Wives of Windsor* turns the tables in a battle that resonates with modern conflicts between the sexes.[33]

In the Henry IV plays female characters are confined to the margins of the action. They make brief appearances at the homes of the rebels in *Part 1*, but no women ever appear at the court of Henry IV, and although Mistress Quickly is the Hostess of the Boar's Head Tavern, she is powerless in the homosocial historical world imagined in the Henry IV plays and *Henry V*, while in *Merry Wives of Windsor*, she is empowered by her membership in the social network of the Windsor community, which includes wives as well as husbands, daughters as well as sons. In the Henry IV plays, although the tavern is designated as hers, it is Falstaff who dominates the tavern scenes and embodies its effeminating pleasures. In these plays, Falstaff is able to appropriate the 'woman's part'. Threatening to corrupt the prince with the temptations of idleness and debauchery, he takes on the role of the amoral, sensual seductress. His contempt for military honour and valour, his loquacity, his lying, his inconstancy, his sensual self-indulgence, his unruly behaviour, and his gross corpulence all implied effeminacy within the system of analogies that opposed spirit to body, aristocrat to plebeian, and man to woman.[34] He refers to his fat belly as a 'womb' (*2 Henry IV*: 4.2.19–20), and he compares himself to a 'sow that hath o'erwhelmed all her litter but one' (*2 Henry IV*: 1.2.9–10). In *Henry IV, Part 1* Falstaff even appropriates what is often considered the most powerful and dangerous of the threats associated with women—that of emasculation. That threat is briefly invoked at the beginning of that play, when Westmoreland reports that the corpses of the English soldiers killed in battle have been abused by Welsh women in a way that 'may not be | Without much shame retold or spoken of' (1.1.45–6). At the end of the play, Falstaff performs what looks like a re-enactment of that reported mutilation when he stabs Hotspur's corpse in the thigh. In Windsor, by contrast, it is Falstaff who suffers a series of symbolic emasculations, all contrived by the women. To cool his lust, he is drenched in a muddy stream. Next, he is dressed in women's clothes and beaten. Finally, he is persuaded to wear the emasculating horns of a cuckold, horns that he intended to plant on the head of Master Ford.

In *The Merry Wives* the women also acquire what was undoubtedly the most important basis of Falstaff's power in the history plays—his theatrical pre-eminence. Here, the characters most closely identified with theatricality are the wives themselves. As the Epilogue to *Henry IV, Part 2* acknowledges, the chief function of any commercial play was entertainment, and in the Henry IV plays Falstaff was the most entertaining figure on stage. 'My fear', the Epilogue begins, 'is your displeasure', and it concludes with a promise to 'continue the story with Sir John in it'. Falstaff is also among the theatrical pleasures promised in the title page of the Quarto edition of *The Merry Wives of Windsor*, which begins by advertising 'A Most pleasaunt and excellent conceited Comedie, of Syr *John Falstaffe*, and the merrie Wives of *Windsor*'. However, the title page also promises to depict the 'pleasing humors' of many other characters: Sir Hugh, the Welsh Knight, Justice Shallow, his wise cousin Master Slender, Ancient Pistol, and Corporal Nym. Here, Falstaff is only one of the many attractions promised by the play. And in the running title—'*A pleasant Comedie, of the merry Wives of Windsor*'—Falstaff disappears. Moreover, in the playscript itself, the characters who are most closely identified with theatrical entertainment are the merry wives, who devise and perform a series of skits for Falstaff's humiliation. Falstaff is featured in these skits, but he does not contrive them, and, unlike the wives, he does not enjoy their performance at all. Although the women offer conventional moral rationales for their actions—that Falstaff needs to be punished, that they want to prove that 'wives may be merry, and yet honest [i.e. chaste] too' (4.2.88–9)—their main purpose is their own entertainment, which, not so incidentally, is the audience's entertainment too.

One crucial difference between a play read and a play seen in the theatre is that the audience in a theatre, having gone there for entertainment, share a communal endeavour and a community of interest and purpose with the characters who are entertainers or enjoying entertainment. Characters like Richard III, Iago, and the witches in *Macbeth* are all attractive on stage. Despite their destructive roles in the represented action, their roles in the production of an entertaining performance are entirely constructive. A novel or a play experienced in solitary reading encourages its readers to imagine themselves into the represented action: their own presence and participation are occluded. A play experienced in the theatre is designed to enlist playgoers in a communal project, which involves the actors who are there to entertain them as well as the characters those actors represent. Clearly, this complicity in the production of theatrical pleasure is part of the appeal of characters who disguise themselves, especially the cross-dressed heroines, such as Rosalind and Viola, who take the audience into their confidence as they deceive the other characters on stage. The women in *The Merry Wives of Windsor* do not themselves adopt male disguise, but they provide a similar pleasure for the audience when they persuade Falstaff to disguise himself from Ford by wearing the clothes of the old woman of Brentford. However, in direct antithesis to the cross-dressed heroines in Shakespeare's other comedies, Falstaff takes no pleasure in his disguise: that privilege is reserved for the wives and for the audience, joined together in a community of laughter from which Falstaff is excluded. At the very end of *The Merry Wives*, Mistress Page includes Falstaff in a general invitation to 'go home, | and laugh this sport o'er by a country fire'. The implication is that he is finally to be included, at least temporarily, in the Windsor community. But for most of the play, he is represented as an isolated figure, betrayed by his followers, scorned by the townspeople, and the solitary butt of their practical jokes.

It is significant that the merry wives, unlike Falstaff, and unlike the heroines of a number of other Shakespearian comedies, do not cross-dress. In plays like *As You Like It*, cross-dressing provides a theatrical holiday for the heroines, temporarily freed from the constraints that define their roles as women in a male-dominated society. In *The Merry Wives of Windsor*, the female characters exercise considerable power in their own persons as women. As such, they provide a striking contrast to what we have come to think of as the paradigmatic Shakespearian heroine, who inhabits a homosocial world where women are isolated and confined within households controlled by fathers and husbands. The merry wives are central figures in the recognizably contemporary Windsor community, and they are empowered by the fact that it includes women as well as men. It may very well be that the oppression and constraints that define the roles of women in the plays we have come to assume as normative were actually counterfactual fantasies rather than reflections of the lives that the majority of Shakespeare's original audience knew outside the theatre.

In the everyday world of Windsor, the only female figure who resembles the heroines of the romantic comedies is Anne Page. She constitutes the centre of a romantic courtship plot, which is conducted in conventional verse rather than the colloquial prose that constitutes the dominant language of the play. Significantly, Anne is characterized from the first as a *representation*. Even before she enters, Slender tells us that 'She has brown hair, and speaks small *like* a woman' (1.1.40–1; my italics). Even her name—Anne Page (an page)—suggests her association with literary and theatrical convention. The romantic heroine disguised as a boy page was a familiar figure to readers and playgoers in Shakespeare's England, and in a few notorious cases actual women followed their example. These cases are often cited in recent scholarship, but it is doubtful that many of the playgoers in Shakespeare's original audiences had ever encountered such a creature in their own lives. Merry wives, however, must have been everywhere.

4

Boys Will Be Girls

Shakespeare's plays have always appealed to women. Many believed that Shakespeare had an uncanny ability to enter into women's minds and hearts and to express their deepest feelings. In the seventeenth century, as we saw in Chapter 3, Margaret Cavendish declared, 'one would think that he had been Metamorphosed from a Man to a Woman'.[1] Three centuries later, Carolyn Heilbrun suggested that Shakespeare 'because the greatest of artists, was the most androgynous of men'.[2] Women have often identified with Shakespeare's female characters and with their predicaments. Many of those characters seemed to offer encouraging role models; many of their stories seemed to imply protests against women's oppression.[3] Shakespeare, according to Mary Cowden Clarke, his first female editor, 'has best asserted women's rights'.[4] Generations of women have found a source for their own empowerment in the power of Shakespeare's writing and in the cultural authority it carried.[5]

In recent years, as we have seen, the validity of these enthusiastic responses has been called into question by arguments that mobilize the authority of history to insist that the original productions of Shakespeare's plays—written by a male author to be performed by an exclusively male company of players—expressed an overwhelmingly masculine point of view. The most compelling of these arguments rest on the fact that the presence of a male body beneath the costume of a female character was never far from the awareness of Shakespeare's original audiences. As Thomas Heywood remarked in his *Apology for Actors* (1612),

To see our youths attired in the habit of women, who knows not what their intents be? Who cannot distinguish them by their names, assuredly knowing, they are but to represent such a lady, at such a time appointed? (C3ᵛ)

Evidence like this seems to discredit the possibility of imagining Shakespeare's female characters as realistic representations of the actual women he knew or exemplary models for future women's empowerment. Nonetheless, the presence of the boy actor—and the audience's awareness of his presence—raises at least as many questions as it seems to close. The implications of transvestite performance in a playhouse where it was customary and a culture in which the modern, Western sex/gender system was not yet in place are by no means transparent.

A case in point is the popular film *Shakespeare in Love* (1998), which highlighted the fact that male actors played women's parts when Shakespeare's plays were first performed but depicted the practice from a distinctly—and anachronistically—modern perspective. In *Shakespeare in Love*, the actor who was cast as Juliet was 'naturally' unable to play the part convincingly; and the players' production of *Romeo and Juliet* did not really come to life until he was replaced by the Lady Viola, disguised as a boy actor, but actually a real woman (and a woman in love to boot) who was herself played by the beautiful Gwyneth Paltrow. In Shakespeare's time, the assumption seems to have been just the opposite. At the beginning of the seventeenth century, Thomas Coryate described his visit to a Venetian playhouse where women performed the female parts:

I saw women act, a thing that I never saw before, though I have heard that it hath been sometimes used in London, and they performed it with as good a grace, action, gesture, and whatsoever convenient for a player, as ever I saw any masculine actor.[6]

Coryate was surprised to see that the women performed the female parts as effectively as the male players he had seen in London. John Downes, as a book keeper and prompter in the Restoration theatre, had seen both male and female actors performing women's parts, but he doubted that any of the women could equal the achievement of Edward Kynaston. Kynaston, he wrote, made a complete female stage beauty, performing his parts so well . . . that it has since been disputable among the judicious, whether any woman that succeeded him so sensibly touched the audience as he.[7]

Responses like these suggest that for early modern playgoers the absence of women from the stage and the use of male actors to play their parts was not regarded as a deficiency and that the male actors' performances of women's parts were regarded as convincing and taken seriously. In our own theatres, by contrast, male cross-dressing invariably threatens to provoke the nervous laughter that arises from contemporary anxieties about masculine sexual identity.

Further evidence that cross-dressed performance was regarded by early modern players as an attraction to be emphasized rather than a deficiency to be concealed can be found in the playscripts themselves, in which cross-dressing was often highlighted. Instead of attempting to conceal the presence of a male actor's body beneath a female character's costume, many of Shakespeare's plays seem clearly designed to exploit it. In three of the most celebrated comedies— *The Merchant of Venice*, *As You Like It*, and *Twelfth Night*—female characters disguise themselves as young men, and their cross-dressed disguise is central to both the complication and the resolution of the plot. The heroines also disguise themselves as men in *The Two Gentlemen of Verona*, one of Shakespeare's earliest plays, and in *Cymbeline*, one of his latest. Shakespeare's playscripts, moreover, contain numerous allusions to the doubly gendered identity of the boy actors who dressed as women to play their parts, even in cases where the female characters do not assume male disguise.

The popularity of cross-dressed characters in the plays of Shakespeare and his contemporaries has attracted widespread scholarly attention in recent years, but these studies have yielded very little consensus in regard to the reasons for their popularity or their implications for early modern understandings of sex and gender. In fact, the debates about their historical implications have made this discourse an arena where our own battles about gender and sexuality are fought. At a time when feminists were challenging the restrictions that limited women's opportunities in our own culture, major feminist scholars often emphasized the liberatory potential of Shakespeare's representations of cross-dressed comic heroines. Male disguise allowed female characters to perform heroic actions that were generally reserved for men. It is only by disguising herself as a man that Portia in *The Merchant of Venice* can act as a lawyer in the Venetian court, where she demonstrates the legal skill that saves Antonio's life after the male characters have been unable to do so. In a pioneering feminist study, Juliet Dusinberre argued that cross-dressed disguise 'freed the dramatist to explore...the natures of women untrammelled by the customs of femininity'.[8] The capacity of cross-dressed performance to destabilize the gender norms of the represented action was also cited in early feminist studies of Shakespearian cross-dressing. We have already seen (in Chapter 3) how the oppressive implications of Kate's performance of submission in *The Taming of the Shrew* are complicated and called into question by reminders in the playscript that her part, like that of Christopher Sly's supposed wife in the Induction, was performed by a boy actor. Moreover, as Catherine Belsey argued, the cross-dressed heroine released 'for the audience the possibility of glimpsing a disruption of sexual difference'.[9]

Other critics offered readings of cross-dressed performance that were much less optimistic for women. Perhaps the most influential of these arguments were those of Stephen Greenblatt and Lisa Jardine (both described in Chapter 1). Greenblatt argued that the point of the cross-dressed disguise in comedies like *Twelfth Night* is that 'men love women precisely as *representations*, a love the original performance of these plays literalized within the person of the boy actor.... The open secret of identity—that within differentiated individuals is a single structure, identifiably male—is presented literally in the all-male cast.'[10] Greenblatt used Thomas Laqueur's theory that there was only 'one sex' in Renaissance anatomical theory and the fact that all the actors on stage were male to theorize a masculinist fantasy of a world without women. Lisa Jardine argued that the spectacle of a boy playing 'the woman's part' was 'an act for a male audience's appreciation'. '[T]hese figures are sexually enticing *qua* transvestied boys', she contended, and 'the plays encourage the audience to view them as such'.[11]

Although Greenblatt identified the appeal of the cross-dressed boys as a version of heteroerotic desire and Jardine insisted that the desire they evoked was homoerotic, both grounded their interpretations on *masculine* erotic desire. What neither seemed to consider is that there were women in the audience as well as men—perhaps, in the view of some theatre historians, more women than men—and the prologues and epilogues to many plays explicitly mark the players' awareness that they needed to please those female play-goers. The Epilogue to *As You Like It*, for instance, addresses both male and female playgoers, but the appeal to the women comes first, and its wording—'I charge you, O women, for the love you bear to men, to like as much of this play as please you'—suggests that the 'you' in the play's title refers primarily to them and that the pleasure it offers them is erotic. As Jean E. Howard has observed, in a theatre 'where men and women alike were both spectacles and spectators, desired and desiring', the women, no less than the men, 'could become desiring subjects' (Howard 1994, pp. 91, 79). Contesting Greenblatt's use of *Twelfth Night* to construct a paradigmatic example of the way erotic desire was directed in Shakespeare's cross-dressed comedies, Valerie Traub argues that although *Twelfth Night* relies on a 'predominantly phallic and visual' erotic economy, 'the erotics of *As You Like It* . . . are diffuse, non-localized, and inclusive . . . [with] provocative affinities with the tactile, contiguous, plural erotics envisioned by Luce Irigaray as more descriptive of female experience' (1992, p. 142).

Conditioned by the assumption that the sexed body is the unshakeable ground of gender identity, we are likely to classify the spectacle of two male actors, both dressed in male attire, kissing or courting on stage, as a performance specifically designed to elicit homoerotic desire in male spectators. However, the tendency of recent scholarship to emphasize the ways the cross-dressed boy might have served as a focus for male homoerotic desire fails to take account of the fact that within the represented action of these plays, it is the women, at least as much as—perhaps more than—the men who desire the cross-dressed heroines. It is also significant that Olivia's infatuation with Cesario and Phoebe's for Rosalind both focus on the *femininity* of the figures they take for young boys. Olivia, who has vowed to remain in seclusion for seven years to mourn her brother's death, abruptly reverses herself and agrees to admit Cesario as soon as Malvolio describes him as an effeminate figure: 'Not yet old enough for a man, nor young enough for a boy . . . he speaks very shrewishly. One would think his mother's milk were scarce out of him' (1.5.139–44). Phoebe describes the object of her desire as a 'pretty youth', 'not very tall', with 'a pretty redness in his lip' (3.5.113–21). The premise underlying these infatuations is that what women naturally desire is not mature, virile men, but effeminate boys whose bodies are more like their own.

This is not to deny that the cross-dressed characters mobilized men's desire as well as women's. Warnings that the boys would inflame male spectators with sodomitical passion were a familiar feature of antitheatrical polemic, and Shakespeare's representations of his cross-dressed heroines seem clearly designed to exploit the homoerotic appeal of a pretty boy. Rosalind stages her entire courtship with Orlando in the person of a boy with the suggestive name of Ganymede. Sebastian, the name adopted by the disguised Julia, and the name of the brother the disguised Viola imitates, had similar implications. In real life, female prostitutes wore male attire to make themselves more alluring to male customers. In 1587, William Harrison wrote, 'I have met some of these trulls in London so disguised that it hath passed my skill to discover whether they were men or women' (p. 147).

As Harrison's indignant report suggests, gender ambiguity itself was regarded as erotically alluring. In Middleton and Dekker's *The Roaring Girl*, the title character, Moll, who dresses in male attire and excels in masculine activities such as swordfighting, is repeatedly slandered as a whore, and she is also depicted as eminently desirable sexually. In this play, unlike *As You Like It* and *Twelfth Night*, none of the female characters is depicted as desiring Moll (most of them, in fact, regard her as a sexual rival); but Laxton, one of the male characters, is delighted at the suggestion that Moll may be 'both man and woman': 'That were excellent', he asserts, 'she might first cuckold the husband, and then make him do as much for the wife' (2.1.221–3). Laxton's reaction is a comic version of the erotic excitement that cross-dressed characters in the plays of Shakespeare and his contemporaries could elicit from both characters and spectators of both sexes. This excitement, like the ambiguous gender identity of the characters themselves, resists analysis in terms of the modern division between homo- and heteroerotic (or even bisexual) desire. It derives from the very ambiguity that those classifications would dismantle.

'Breeches parts' were enormously popular on the post-Restoration stage, where the actresses who performed the roles of the disguised boys could put their actual, sexed bodies on display for the pleasure of male spectators.[12] Instead of disturbing the gender identity of the cross-dressed heroines, these performances insisted on its stability by emphasizing the femininity of the female characters, unchanged by their male attire. In the context of a sex/gender system increasingly grounded in biology, the spectacle of a woman's body in male attire reassuringly emphasized that the sexed body persisted beneath the otherwise gendered clothes. But even in Shakespeare's time, when the modern, biologically grounded sex-gender system was only beginning to take shape and the use of boys to play women's parts seems to suggest that gender divisions were not yet fixed in the ground of differently sexed bodies, similar implications appear in a number of playtexts. From this distance, it is difficult to read those implications with total assurance, just as we cannot surely know what Jacobean women had in mind when they adopted masculine fashions. Although there was no law against cross-dressing, men's clothing had long been regulated by law to ensure that it would not misrepresent their social status and identity. Given the importance of clothing as a signifier of social status, we might assume that these women were attempting to challenge the constraints implicit in their identities as women. At the same time, however, since social gender was increasingly rationalized as the product of a biologically sexed body, they may have been wearing male attire to reveal their essentially and unchangingly female sexed bodies as a temptation for male erotic desire. In 1620, the misogynist pamphlet *Hic Mulier or The Man-Woman* described the woman in masculine attire as wearing a 'loose, lascivious ... French doublet, being all unbuttoned to entice ... and extreme short waisted to give a most easy way to every luxurious action' (1985, p. 267).

Although recent criticism has been understandably fascinated by the erotic excitement activated by cross-dressed heroines, it is difficult to read the nature and directions of the erotic feelings mobilized under a sexual regime that was strikingly different from our own. Moreover, despite the fact that there is considerable evidence for the erotic excitement generated by cross-dressing, it was probably not the only reason for the popularity of cross-dressed heroines in the plays of

Shakespeare and his contemporaries. A remarkable number of plays featured them. Michael Shapiro lists eighty in the appendix to his book *Gender in Play on the Shakespearean Stage*, but his list does not claim to be exhaustive, and it is impossible to know exactly how many there were.[13] One traditional explanation for their popularity seems to rest on the same anachronistically modern assumption we saw in *Shakespeare in Love*: Shakespeare put his heroines into male disguise, it was claimed, because it was easier for the boy actors to play as boys. This explanation never made much sense because most of Shakespeare's female characters, including such demanding roles as Lady Macbeth and Cleopatra, never take on male disguises. Moreover, a boy portraying a female character disguised as a boy would probably have performed in subtly different ways from a boy portraying a character who was actually a boy, so the double-cross is likely to have been even more difficult to perform than the straightforward impersonation of a woman. A more likely explanation, which acknowledges the well-documented skill and effectiveness of the boy actors, is that the disguise gave them additional opportunities to put their virtuosity on display. The kind of seamless, unbroken dramatic illusion demanded by the post-Shakespearian classic realist theatre was clearly not a requirement in a theatre where actors frequently stepped forward to address the audience directly in asides and soliloquies that explicitly acknowledged the present reality of dramatic presentation. When female characters took on male disguise, the ambiguous gender identity of the actors who played their parts could be advertised in the performance, calling attention to the actors' virtuosity and inviting the playgoers to admire their accomplishment. The cross-dressed boy, in fact, could be used to celebrate the mystery of theatrical impersonation, which enabled both the represented character and the representing actor to be simultaneously present to the audience in the artful person of a single performer.

In Shakespeare's England, the craft of the professional players was still a novelty. The first purpose-built professional playhouse, the Red Lion, was not erected until 1567, and although the London playing companies rapidly developed a remarkable degree of professionalism, they were still not numbered among the professional guilds that organized the more traditional crafts. The novelty of the actors' trade provoked numerous attacks. Antitheatrical invective typically charged that dramatic impersonation was a form of deceit, the players misrepresenting their true identities. The deceitfulness of play-acting was repeatedly conflated in these attacks with the deceitfulness of dressing in real life in clothing that rightly belonged to someone of a higher status or different sex.[14] A frequently quoted example is Stephen Gosson's charge, 'In Stage Plays for a boy to put on the attire, the gesture, the passions of a woman; for a mean person to take upon him the title of a Prince with counterfeit port, and train, is by outward signs to show themselves otherwise than they are, and so within the compass of a lie.'[15] Gosson's citation of the cross-dressed boy as a prime exhibit in his attack is typical of antitheatrical polemic.

Many playscripts encode the players' awareness of these attacks, reproducing the antitheatrical charges in order to satirize or refute them. A case in point is Shakespeare's *The Two Gentlemen of Verona*, in which the fickle, deceitful lover is named Proteus, and Julia, the faithful lady he abandons, is the first of Shakespeare's cross-dressed comic heroines. Proteus, the shape-shifting god of classical antiquity, was used by both admirers and detractors of the players as a prototype for their craft of impersonation.[16] Shakespeare himself used Proteus as a prototype of wicked deceit in *Henry VI, Part 3*, when the future Richard III boasts to the audience about his ability to deceive, claiming that he 'can add colours to the chameleon' and 'change shapes with Proteus for advantages' (3.2.191–2). At the same time, the terms Richard uses to describe his virtuosity as a deceiver were also used by the players' admirers to celebrate their artistry. Both Edward Alleyn and Richard Burbage, the actor who first played Richard's part, were compared by enthusiastic contemporaries to Proteus. In *The Two Gentlemen of Verona* Shakespeare's portrait of the character he called Proteus as a treacherous deceiver seems to echo the players' detractors; but the play also offers a defence of theatrical impersonation, which is provided by the cross-dressed lady that Proteus has betrayed.

In an often-cited dialogue at the end of Act 4, Julia, disguised as the boy Sebastian, is asked whether (s)he knows Julia. Gesturing towards the duplicity of both the character's and the player's identity, the supposed boy replies that 'he' knows her '[a]lmost as well as I do know myself' and that he has 'wept a hundred several times' while 'think[ing] upon her woes' (4.4.135–7). Asked how tall Julia is, 'Sebastian' replies that they are so close in height that he was able to wear her gown in a pageant when he played 'the woman's part' (4.4.149–55), a claim that might have reminded Shakespeare's original audience that the same boy actor who was now dressed as the boy Sebastian had earlier taken on 'the woman's part' of Julia by wearing her gown. This reminder would have carried extra weight for Elizabethan playgoers even if they were not familiar with the antitheatrical objections to boy players taking women's parts, for they were all subject to the sumptuary laws that regulated men's dress to ensure that it did not misrepresent their social identity. Most important, in a theatre where parts were habitually doubled, any change of costume was inevitably read as a change of identity (Hooper 1915; Jones and Stallybrass 2000, pp. 193–206).

The supposed boy's description of his cross-dressed performance in the pageant, with Julia herself as one of the spectators, conjures up a *tour de force* of layered impersonation—the boy actor, impersonating Julia, who impersonates a boy, who claims to have impersonated a woman in a pageant in which he wore Julia's dress to play the part of Ariadne, abandoned by Theseus,

> Which I so lively acted with my tears
> That my poor mistress, movèd therewithal,
> Wept bitterly; and would I might be dead
> If I in thought felt not her very sorrow.
> (4.4.161–4)

This dizzying whirl of identification—Julia is Sebastian is Ariadne—is resolved only when Julia's sympathetic response to the performance unites actor and spectator in imagined sorrow and real tears. The description invites the playgoers' admiration, both by calling attention to the player's art of impersonation and by modelling the response of a sympathetic spectator.

Julia's cross-dressing in this early play rehearses themes that would be more fully developed in later plays. The same combination of layered, cross-gendered impersonation and solicitation of the playgoers' admiration reappears in the Epilogue to *As You Like It*, where the indeterminate gender identity of the cross-dressed heroine is again featured in an advertisement for the players' craft. The Epilogue is spoken by the actor who plays Rosalind, who is the most attractive figure in the cast, not only because her/his sexual ambiguity is itself erotically exciting, but also because of her/his explicit theatricality. Both of these qualities are explicitly featured in the flirtatious Epilogue, which insists that the speaker is both Rosalind and the male actor who played her part. At the beginning of the speech, the speaker seems to be the female character, when she says, 'It is not the fashion to see the lady the epilogue'. Later in the same speech, however, it is the male actor who played her part who offers, 'If I were a woman I would kiss as many of you as had beards that pleased me, complexions that liked me, and breaths that I defied not.' But this is not the end, for (s)he quickly adds, 'And I am sure, as many as have good beards, or good faces, or sweet breaths will for my kind offer, when I make curtsy, bid me farewell.' At this point— the last lines in the playtext, which were presumably followed by a curtsy—the gender of the speaker becomes completely indeterminate, as the audience is invited to applaud. The *tour de force* of a boy actor portraying a woman who takes on the disguise and role of a boy makes that doubly gendered figure the embodiment of the erotic excitement, the duplicity and the dazzle of the entire theatrical performance.

Most of the recent scholarship on Shakespeare's cross-dressed heroines has focused on the comedies—understandably so, since none of the female characters in his tragedies and histories takes on the disguise of a man. Moreover in those plays, the characters who are most explicitly and memorably associated with the figure of the actor are all men. In the histories and tragedies, both the glamour and the moral ambivalence of theatrical impersonation are most memorably and directly embodied in such figures as Richard III, Falstaff, and Iago. The only exception is Cleopatra. Cleopatra alludes at one often-cited point in the play (2.5.21–3) to exchanging clothing with Antony, but she never appears in male clothing or takes on the disguise of a man. Nonetheless, she is the only other Shakespearian heroine who rivals Rosalind in theatrical power and allure, and she is also the only tragic heroine who explicitly calls attention to the fact that her part was performed by a boy actor.

Cleopatra is also one of only three female characters whose names are featured in the titles of Shakespeare's plays, and of those three she is the only one who has a greater role in the dramatic action than the male character with whom her name is paired. Antony dies at the end of Act IV, but it is not until the end of Act V, after Cleopatra's suicide, that the play reaches its conclusion. Like Rosalind, Cleopatra dominates the represented action, repeatedly upstaging the other characters. Instead of maintaining a decorous womanly silence, she speaks about 20 per cent of the words in the entire script, and, as Ania Loomba has observed, 'she also controls the speech of others. Even Antony is unable to break into her speech and get a word in.'[17] The third scene of the play begins with a dialogue in which every one of Antony's speeches is cut short by Cleopatra's interruption (1.3.23–31). Even in Antony's final scene, she interrupts him: dying, Antony asks, 'Give me some wine, and let me speak a little.' 'No', Cleopatra responds, 'let me speak' (4.16.44–5). In addition, Cleopatra frequently dominates even those scenes when she is absent from the stage, as the other characters repeatedly speculate about her effect on Antony. A case in point is Act II, scene ii. Cleopatra is not physically present on stage, but Enobarbus's eloquent description of her appearance when she first displayed herself to Antony at Cydnus produces what is certainly, with the sole exception of her suicide, Cleopatra's most magnificent representation in the entire play. Cleopatra also dominates the plot. The rift between Antony and Caesar is motivated by his allegiance to Cleopatra, as is his loss of the decisive Battle of Actium and his subsequent suicide. Finally, it is Cleopatra who inflicts on Caesar the only defeat he suffers during the course of the play, first tricking him into believing she wants to preserve her life, and then arranging the spectacular death that changes what was to be his triumph into hers.

Of all Shakespeare's heroines, Cleopatra most fully embodies the paradoxical implications of transvestite performance, even though she never appears on stage in male disguise. She is Shakespeare's most compelling image of female erotic power at the same time that she is also the only one of his tragic heroines whose lines explicitly refer to the boy actor who played her part. Explaining to her women why she cannot allow herself to be taken to Rome, she predicts,

> The quick comedians
> Extemporally will stage us, and present
> Our Alexandrian revels. Antony
> Shall be brought drunken forth, and I shall see
> Some squeaking Cleopatra boy my greatness
> I' th' posture of a whore.
>
> (5.2.212–17)

Cleopatra's description of the deceptive, debauched, and degraded staging she anticipates at the hands of the Roman comedians closely echoes the charges that were levelled against the players in Shakespeare's England, and it also seems to validate those charges because the treatment she anticipates would surely have reminded Shakespeare's original audiences of the treatment she was receiving in their own playhouse, where the word *boy* had an immediate and obvious application to the actor who spoke these lines, where Antony had been shown in drunken revelry, and where Cleopatra had indeed appeared in the posture of a whore. However, although *Antony and Cleopatra* associates the cross-dressed boy actor with the deceptiveness and degradation that were associated by the enemies of the theatre with play-acting, it also uses that same figure to celebrate the players' art. Here, as in *The Two Gentlemen of Verona* and *As You Like It*, the reference to the boy actor alludes to the present theatrical performance, but here its implications are both more complicated and more central to the represented action. While the references to the boy actors in the earlier plays invited the playgoers' admiration for their virtuosity, the reference in *Antony and Cleopatra* suggests that the boy actor can offer only a poor parody of the character he purports to represent. At the same time, this speech also clears the ground for a defence of Cleopatra—and of the players—against the very charges it seems to endorse, for it opens a rift between the represented character and the representing actor that calls everything the audience has seen so far into question. Insisting on the disparity between the dramatic spectacle and the reality it has attempted to represent, the speech implies that the very performance the audience has seen so far was misleading, but in so doing it prepares the way for a new performance that will show Cleopatra in a radically different guise.

Here, as in the earlier plays, the debate about the theatre is still centred in the figure of the boy actor, but in *Antony and Cleopatra* the antitheatrical case is much more fully laid out, and the issues it raises are much less easy to resolve. The debate about the theatre is thematized in the central dramatic conflict between Rome and Egypt and in Cleopatra's contradictory behaviour, for the ambivalent status of theatrical performance seems to be personified in the ambivalence of Cleopatra's characterization. In a very important sense, the entire play turns on the question of the worth of shows, which is also the question of the worth of Antony's Egyptian queen. Cleopatra is nothing if not theatrical, but instead of the simple dichotomy between negative deceit and positive illusion that was projected into two separate characters in *Two Gentlemen of Verona*, the antithetical claims are both embodied in a single—and singularly ambivalent—character. Cleopatra, like Proteus, is characterized as a deceiver, and her detractors denounce her in terms that closely echo contemporary denunciations of the players. At the same time, like Julia—and also like Rosalind in *As You Like It*—Cleopatra also demonstrates the beneficent power of theatrical performance. Even as she exemplifies precisely those failings for which the enemies of the theatre denounced the players, she also exemplifies the attractions for which the players were admired. She is arguably Shakespeare's most profound and powerful exploration of the ambivalence of the player's craft.

That Cleopatra is designed to be seen as a kind of player is apparent from the opening scene, when she tells the audience, 'I'll seem the fool I am not'—a remark that serves as a pithy announcement of the role she will play in the subsequent action. Like the shape-shifting god Proteus and like the chameleons to which contemporary players were also compared, she will be constant only in constantly changing. Her strategy in love is to present a series of shows in order to keep Antony unsure of her feelings and motivations, but in most of the play, the audience is also unsure, as is demonstrated by the sharply divided critical estimates of her character and motivation. Significantly, she never has a soliloquy; but behind her spectacular parade of shifting moods and stratagems—the magnificent inconstancy that Enobarbus celebrates as 'infinite variety'—one motive remains constant: from beginning to end, she is a dedicated contriver of shows. Some of Cleopatra's shows are obviously trivial—'play' in both senses of the word—as when she changes clothes with Antony or has a salt fish hung on his fishing line, or acts as his armourer. Others are more calculated stratagems, contrived to ensure her hold over Antony:

> See where he is, who's with him, what he does.
> I did not send you. If you find him sad,
> Say I am dancing; if in mirth, report
> That I am sudden sick.
>
> (1.3.2–5)

Enobarbus's description of her initial seduction of Antony emphasizes that it too was a kind of show—a carefully calculated theatrical display, complete with elaborate costumes, a spectacular set, supporting actors dressed to resemble mythological figures, and a musical accompaniment. As Enobarbus five times reiterates, the entire spectacle was a marvel of seeming. Her barge was '*like* a burnished throne', the pretty boys who fanned Cleopatra were '*like* smiling Cupids', the wind they made 'did *seem* to glow the delicate cheeks which they did cool', the gentlewomen who attended Cleopatra were '*like* the Nereides', and the helmsman was 'a *seeming* mermaid' (2.2.196–215). Enobarbus's admiring description casts him in the role of a delighted playgoer, fully aware that the spectacle he saw was a show, but thrilled by its glorious contrivance. At the end of the play, Cleopatra contrives a similar show for the audience in the spectacular suicide that inflicts on Caesar the only defeat he suffers in the course of the play. In that scene even Caesar is captivated by Cleopatra's magnificent display. 'She looks like sleep', he declares, 'As she would catch another Antony | In her strong toil of grace' (5.2.336–8).

Cleopatra's critics within the play make the same kind of charges against her that antitheatrical writers were levelling against the players and their customers. She is deceptive and immoral. Her seductions corrupt Antony. The time he spends with her in Egypt is wasted in idleness and debauchery, which compromise his manhood. There is ample evidence in the playtext to support all of these charges. Antony's mismanagement of his military and political affairs, his repeated vacillations between Egypt and Rome, and his bungled suicide all support the Romans' charge that his 'lascivious wassails' (1.5.56) in Egypt have transformed him from 'the triple pillar of the world | Into a strumpet's fool' (1.1.12–13). Cleopatra's own words often lend credence to these charges. She describes her seduction of Antony as a kind of betrayal, like catching fish:

> I will betray
> Tawny-finned fishes. My bended hook shall pierce
> Their slimy jaws, and as I draw them up
> I'll think them every one an Antony
> And say 'Ah ha, you're caught!'
>
> (2.5.11–15)

She luxuriates in masturbatory reveries. Imagining Antony on his horse, she declares, 'O happy horse, to bear the weight of Antony!' (1.5.21). She invites her servants (and the audience along with them) to

> Think on me,
> That am with Phoebus' amorous pinches black,
> And wrinkled deep in time. Broad-fronted Caesar,
> When thou wast here above the ground I was
> A morsel for a monarch, and great Pompey
> Would stand and make his eyes grow in my brow.
> There would he anchor his aspect, and die [i.e. reach a sexual climax]
> With looking on his life.
>
> (1.5.27–34)

In direct contrast to the nubile, cross-dressed heroines of Shakespeare's earlier comedies, his Cleopatra is past the prime of youth. Coupled with the reference to her sun-blackened and age-wrinkled appearance, these vivid recollections of former sexual partners might easily conjure up the repellent image of an ageing whore; and in fact, Cleopatra easily admits that she is one of those 'that trade in love' (2.5.2). With all this evidence—and more—George Bernard Shaw summed up the case against Cleopatra, and against the play as well:

I always think of what Dr. Johnson said: 'Sir, the long and short of it is, the woman's a whore!' You can't feel any sympathy for Antony after.... Actium ... All Shakespear's rhetoric and pathos cannot reinstate Antony after that, or leave us with a single good word for his woman.[18]

The fact that the agent of the hero's fall is an immoral, seductive woman would have had additional resonance at the beginning of the seventeenth century, when Antony's corruption would have been associated with the potential corruption of the theatre audience itself. In contemporary arguments against the theatre, the dangerous effects of playgoing were inscribed in the same register as the dangerous power of women's erotic allure. The sexual seductiveness and deceptiveness of women were proverbial, and these same evils were repeatedly ascribed to the players. William Rankins compared the seductive allure of the players to that of the sirens singing to Ulysses, the temptations they offered to those of an Egyptian concubine.[19] The debauchery and idleness associated with playgoing were also implicated in the lexicon of misogyny, because both of these vices were coded as a loss of manhood. Caesar describes Antony's corruption in exactly those terms: because he 'fishes, drinks, and wastes | The lamps of night in revel', Antony 'is not more manlike | Than Cleopatra, nor the queen of Ptolemy | More womanly than he' (1.4.4–7). Cleopatra makes the same connection when she recalls how she drank Antony 'to his bed, | Then put my tires and mantles on him whilst | I wore his sword' (2.5.21–3). Cleopatra's effect on Antony, like that of the playhouse on its male customers, is to compromise manhood in lustful pleasure.

But if Cleopatra exemplifies the vices and dangers for which the players were condemned, she also exemplifies the attractions that made them so successful. Even at her most reprehensible, she is always entertaining, and before the play ends she will redeem her character in a spectacular show of magnificence that celebrates the transformative potential of the player's art. Cleopatra's suicide and her preparation for it are—and are represented as—triumphs of showmanship. On stage, they are calculated to delight an audience. In the represented action, they are depicted as a series of shows that deceive Caesar and defeat him in what is defined throughout as a contest of showmanship. Caesar's motivation throughout Act V is to keep Cleopatra alive so he can display her in Rome as his prisoner in a show that will celebrate his triumphant victory. As he explains in the opening scene of Act V, 'her life in Rome | Would be eternal in our triumph' (5.1.65–6). Closely guarded to keep her from committing suicide, Cleopatra nonetheless contrives to stage the shows that deceive Caesar and thwart his purpose, ensuring that the spectacular triumph the audience sees on stage at the end of the play takes place in Egypt, not Rome, and that it is not Caesar's triumph but her own apotheosis.

At the beginning of Act V, Cleopatra's character is still ambiguous. Antony has just killed himself as a result of her deception—the false report she sent of her own suicide. In the very next scene after his death, she seems to be attempting to strike a bargain with Caesar, sending a submissive message asking for 'instruction | that she may frame herself | To the way she's forced to' (5.1.54–6). Next, she promises that if Caesar will give her the Egypt she admits he has conquered for her son, she will 'kneel to him with thanks' (5.2.18–21). She gives every indication that she is determined to preserve both herself and her treasure by coming to ignominious terms with her conqueror. She summons her treasurer to verify her claim that she has given Caesar a full account of her wealth. When the treasurer reveals that she has kept back at least half, she flies into a rage, extravagantly denouncing and threatening him and just as extravagantly begging Caesar's pity and indulgence. At this point, Caesar seems to be fully in control of the action. He has defeated Antony, conquered Egypt, and captured Cleopatra, and she seems to be taken in by his deceitful promise that he will treat her as a friend. It is not until Caesar leaves the stage that Cleopatra reveals that it is not she but Caesar who has been deceived. She turns to her women and says, 'He words me, girls,…that I should not be noble to myself' (5.2.187–8), thus revealing that she has only pretended to trust Caesar. She also reveals that it is she, not Caesar, who will control the remainder of the action. She says, 'I have spoke already, and it is provided', 'it' being the basket of figs that is the necessary prop for the final show by which she will dramatize her nobility and Antony's.

That Cleopatra's suicide is designed as a show would be apparent in performance. She even changes costume for it onstage. 'Show me, my women, like a queen', she says, 'Go fetch my best attires' (5.2.223–4). Much is made of dressing; in fact, Charmian's dying gesture is to straighten the dead queen's crown. Her words, 'Your crown's awry. | I'll mend it and then play' (5.2.308–9), echo Cleopatra's order for the costume: 'when thou hast done this chore I'll give thee leave | To play till doomsday.—Bring our crown and all' (5.2.227–8). The word *play* emphasizes both the hedonism and the theatricality of the death Cleopatra and her women are staging, but the fact that the crown is their repeated concern ennobles that theatricality by actualizing it in the iconic symbol of royalty. Until this point in the play, Cleopatra has behaved more like a quean than a queen. She has physically assaulted a messenger, chasing him around the stage; indulged in wild exhibitions of rage and grief; openly displayed her eroticism, and shamefully humbled herself before Caesar. But now she visually redefines herself as royal, for she has put on the crown, which is the essential theatrical emblem of royalty.

Cleopatra commands her women to 'show' her 'like a queen', but both for the characters onstage and for the audience, that likeness becomes reality. The audience sees her dressed in royal regalia and wearing the crown, and the word 'royal' echoes like a refrain in the closing lines of the play. After Cleopatra dies, Charmian says, 'golden Phoebus never be beheld | Of eyes again so royal' (5.2.307–8). When Caesar's guard enters to discover the dead queen, he asks (in terms that might apply equally well to a theatrical performance), 'Is this well done?'; and Charmian replies, 'It is well done, and fitting for a princess | Descended of so many royal kings' (5.2.317–18). Discovering Cleopatra's death, Caesar realizes that 'she levelled at our purposes, and, being royal, | Took her own way' (5.2.326–7). Of these lines, only the interchange with the guard appears in Shakespeare's source, Sir Thomas North's translation of Plutarch's *Life of Antony*, and North's adjective is 'noble'.

In Cleopatra's suicide scene, the question of Cleopatra's worth is directly associated with the question of the worth of shows. The 'squeaking boy' speech seems to set the two at odds: only if the playgoers reject the show they have been watching can they accept the unseen greatness of the character the boy could not truly represent. It also seems to anticipate the modern view of transvestite performance that was dramatized in *Shakespeare in Love*. Without an actress to play her part, it seems to imply, Cleopatra cannot be truly represented on stage. In the remainder of the scene, however, Cleopatra—still impersonated by a boy actor—stages a new show that redefines her character as the protagonist of a high tragedy. When Cleopatra contracts for a moment to the 'squeaking boy' who acted her part on Shakespeare's stage and reminds the audience that everything they have seen and heard so far is part of a show, she prepares the way for a new show that displays her virtuosity as a performer and that of the boy actor who played her part—the spectacular suicide scene that will validate both her own worth and the worth of theatrical performance.

What the audience sees in Cleopatra's suicide is an act that is explicitly marked as theatrical. In a play, a queen can put on her royalty with its emblems. The costume she wears, the poetry she speaks, and the act she performs satisfy the only truth-criteria that are available within the context of the stage. Having assumed her royal regalia, Cleopatra proceeds to act the part of a queen, explicitly renouncing all the faults that defined her character in the earlier parts of the play. Then she could outdrink Antony; now she renounces the grape. Then she was Antony's strumpet; now she claims the title of his wife. Ever 'a boggler' (3.13.111), she will now be 'marble-constant'. To claim this monumental perfection, however, she also renounces her sex: 'My resolution's placed', she declares,

> and I have nothing
> Of woman in me. Now from head to foot
> I am marble-constant. Now the fleeting moon
> No planet is of mine.
>
> (5.2.234–7)

In this final renunciation, Cleopatra seems to admit what the Romans within the play and the enemies of the theatre outside it had implied all along—that all her defects were intrinsic to her gender. But she does not renounce her sex in order to collapse into the squeaking boy who played her part any more than her rejection of the shows the boy put on meant that she was done with showing. Her sex, like her showmanship, is not erased in this final scene but sublimated. Even her sexuality remains: 'the stroke of death is as a lover's pinch, which hurts and is desired' (5.2.286–7); and the deadly asp is like a 'baby at [her] breast, | That sucks the nurse asleep' (5.2.300–1). What makes this redefinition of her character credible is that she has already called into question all the evidence that went to build the case against her. Her reference to the squeaking Cleopatra who would have boyed her greatness in Rome claims for the represented character a greatness beyond anything that the audience has so far seen on the stage, where her part was indeed played by a boy.

Clearly, Shakespeare's Cleopatra was originally conceived as a role for a male actor. But her character was also shaped by an ancient tradition that conceived the fabled Egyptian queen in distinctly female terms. To the Romans, she was notorious as 'the harlot queen'.[20] To Boccaccio, she was 'an object of gossip for the whole world' for her beauty, her lust for power and riches, and her sexual licence (*De Claris Mulieribus*, quoted in Hamer, pp. 30–1). Shakespeare's play both drew on that pre-existing tradition and reworked it, with the result that Cleopatra's form in the post-Shakespearian cultural imagination has been largely shaped by his version of her character. However, although the issue of theatricality is never far from the surface in Shakespeare's version of the story, the issue of gender has tended to dominate in subsequent commentary, in which she typically serves 'as a kind of synecdoche or epitome of the feminine'.[21] For men, Cleopatra has often represented a distinctively female threat, defined by the Romans' account of her corrupting and effeminizing effect on Antony. Dr Johnson expressed his own sense of the magnitude of the threat represented by Cleopatra when he described 'the quibble' (i.e. pun) as 'the fatal Cleopatra for which [Shakespeare] lost the world, and was content to lose it'. For Johnson, who was a great neoclassical moralist and lexicographer as well as a passionate admirer of Shakespeare, Shakespeare's quibbles were a matter of grave importance. They had 'some malignant power over his mind, and [their] fascinations [were] irresistible'. 'A quibble ... gave him such delight, that he was content to purchase it, by the sacrifice of reason, propriety, and truth.'[22] Just as Antony, the greatest soldier in Rome, had been corrupted by his irresistible attraction to a woman who was the embodiment of moral ambiguity, the language of Shakespeare, the greatest writer in English, was corrupted by his fascination with linguistic ambiguity.

As Carol Cook has observed, Johnson was only the first of many writers who have invoked the figure of Cleopatra to describe the subversive potential of language to disrupt the categories of thought, although in the hands of twentieth-century writers, such as Hélène Cixous, this 'feminine practice of writing' has often been cause for celebration (Cook, pp. 241–3). These, like other post-Shakespearian responses to Cleopatra, have been fractured by the same ambivalence that characterizes the divided responses to her by the other characters in Shakespeare's play; but admirers and detractors alike have seen her as Shakespeare's conception of a quintessentially female personality. She has pride of place as the first character mentioned in the first published piece of Shakespeare criticism, in which she exemplifies what Margaret Cavendish regarded as Shakespeare's preternatural ability to describe women as they truly were.[23] Again and again, she has been described as Shakespeare's image of 'the archetypal woman': to Swinburne, she was 'Blake's Eternal Female', to Georg Brandes, 'woman of women, quintessential Eve'. S. L. Bethell found that 'In Cleopatra [Shakespeare] presents the mystery of woman'. As Linda Fitz (Woodbridge) has observed, these, and many other, male writers have typically depicted Shakespeare's Cleopatra in terms of misogynist stereotypes, as a 'practiser of feminine wiles, mysterious, childlike, long on passion and short on intelligence—except for a sort of animal cunning'. E. E. Stoll, for instance, concluded that she was 'quintessential woman' because '[c]aprice, conscious and unconscious is her nature'.[24] If male critics have often been threatened by the combination of political power and erotic attraction that Cleopatra represents, those same attributes have just as often appealed to women as an emblem of their own desires for empowerment. As Irene Dash explained, Shakespeare's Cleopatra 'suggests the potential for women if they could have self-sovereignty and function as complete people, not in a sexless world or a world, where, like Queen Elizabeth, they must choose between marriage and career, but in a world where true mutuality might exist between men and women'.[25]

The fact that Shakespeare embodied his most powerful celebration of the player's art in the person of a female character has allowed his Cleopatra to become a figure of empowerment for subsequent women, even though her most powerful moment in his play cannot be staged until she reminds the audience that her part was performed by a boy. As an image of archetypal woman represented in the figure of a boy actor, Shakespeare's Cleopatra epitomizes the paradox of all theatrical representation, which is both compromised and perfected by the actor's mediation. Dramatic characters are present on stage only as they are embodied in the actors who play their parts. Cleopatra's reference to the boy actor who played her part makes explicit the fact that femininity on Shakespeare's stage was always a show to be performed. As a supremely resourceful playwright, Shakespeare exploited all the materials of production at his disposal, including the use of boys to play women's roles. This does not mean, however, that their representations have nothing to say to women. As Dympna

Callaghan has observed, the fact 'that Cleopatra is so compelling a *female* character role written for a male actor' reminds us that '[t]he crude category of woman, defined only by biology and outside the text and insulated from the ways in which cultural representations produce and reinforce assigned subject positions, is a classification of no more substantial existence than the most outlandish fiction'. This is not to say that the word 'woman' has no meaning or that the concept it denotes has no impact in the actual world. As Callaghan also insists, the fact that the category of 'woman' is 'bound up with representation renders...[it] no less real'.[26] All of Shakespeare's female characters were designed for transvestite performance, and yet they still possess an enormous cultural power to define our notions of women's roles in life. The enduring allure of the show of femininity that was performed in their names continues to shape, over four centuries later, what it means to act like a woman.

The Lady's Reeking Breath

Shakespeare's plays tell us both too much and too little about his views of women. Female characters are idealized and demonized, and behaviour that elicits praise and success in some contexts is condemned and punished in others. Most important, every word in the playscripts was written as the utterance of a character, whose views do not necessarily coincide with those of their author. The sonnets, by contrast, were written in the first person, tempting many readers to look there for autobiographical disclosures. William Wordsworth, for instance, famously declared, 'with this key [i.e. the sonnet] Shakespeare unlocked his heart'.

The temptation to search the sonnets for personal revelations might seem especially compelling in regard to Shakespeare's attitudes towards women not only because here, unlike the playscripts, the woman is described in the poet's own voice but also because her representation is not mediated by the presence of a male actor performing her part. Even in the sonnets, however, the effects of mediation are everywhere apparent, for a long tradition of literary production had already established the conventions that defined both the writer's task and his original readers' expectations.

The fourteenth-century Italian humanist Francesco Petrarca was not the first poet to employ the sonnet form, but his *Rime in Vita e Morta di Madonna Laura* set the terms of what came to be known as the Petrarchan sonnet, a genre that enjoyed a remarkable popularity in France and England during the sixteenth century. It has been estimated that over three hundred thousand sonnets were produced in Europe during that period. Petrarch's sonnets were not arranged in a narrative sequence, but they did tell a kind of story, since most of them described the poet's devotion to an idealized lady whom he called Laura—a devotion that persisted after her death. In addition to setting the sonnet form of fourteen lines, divided into an eight-line octave followed by a six-line sestet, Petrarch's sonnets also defined the roles and characterization of the sonneteer and his lady. She, like Laura, was idealized and unattainable; he, like Petrarch, was an all-too-human figure who suffered the greatest torments in the throes of his passion.

Although Petrarch wrote three hundred and seventeen sonnets, he never provided a detailed portrait of Laura. To this day, it is still not known whether she actually existed. Some of Petrarch's friends thought that 'Laura' was merely a fictitious name, chosen to signal the 'laurels' that Petrarch finally achieved in 1341 when he was crowned Poet Laureate in Rome; and in fact, the sonnets contain numerous puns on 'Laura' and the Italian and Latin words for 'laurel'. Petrarch, however, insisted that she was a real woman, although he never identified her. In any event, the Laura of his sonnets never emerges as a human personality. As Nancy Vickers has observed, she 'is always presented as a part or parts of a woman. . . . her image is that of a collection of exquisitely beautiful dissociated objects'.[1]

Idealized, but also objectified and dehumanized, Petrarch's Laura became the model for the ladies celebrated in subsequent sonnet sequences. Although the names of the ladies varied, they shared the same essential Petrarchan attributes and they were described in images that quickly became conventional. Because the Petrarchan lady was fair, her beauty could be compared to the light of heavenly bodies or at the very least to precious earthly objects such as gold and pearls. Because she was unattainable, she could represent a Neoplatonic ideal and the lover's passion could be sublimated into self-transcendence. Some of the ladies may have truly had those attributes; some of the poets (along with their readers) may have sought out ladies who had them; many of the poets undoubtedly constructed their ladies out of whole cloth. None of this really matters: what was important was the attributes, not the ladies.

Michael Drayton's sonnets may have been addressed to a lady named Anne Goodere, but the title of his collection, *Idea's Mirror* (1594), associated his lady with the Platonic idea of perfection. Sir Philip Sidney's sonnets were ostensibly addressed to Penelope Rich, but he named them *Astrophil* [i.e. star-lover] *and Stella* [star] (1591, 1598). The lady in this tradition is never so much a human personality as an occasion for metaphors and for the poet's own performance of various actions that are important to him. Perhaps most important of all was the act of writing itself, for which the lady served as the inspiration. Purportedly designed to win or to immortalize the lady, the sonnets were also and always designed to immortalize the poet, and he was always the central character. The lady was simply an occasion for the poet's varied states of mind and spirit. Sometimes the poets suffered, sometimes they exulted or ascended from earthly love to spiritual self-transcendence, but at every stage they described and analysed their feelings in loving, metaphorical detail. The lady may have been the object of the poet's devotion, but the subject of the sonnets was the poet himself.

Shakespeare seems to recognize the essential narcissism of the Petrarchan conventions in the scene in *King John* where John and the French king Philip arrange a politically expedient marriage between John's niece Blanche and Philip's son, Louis the Dauphin. Having been asked by the two kings whether he can love the lady, the Dauphin replies,

> . . . in her eye I find
> A wonder, or a wondrous miracle,
> The shadow of myself formed in her eye;
> Which, being but the shadow of your son,
> Becomes a sun and makes your son a shadow.
> I do protest I never loved myself
> Till now enfixèd I beheld myself
> Drawn in the flattering table of her eye.
>
> (2.1.497–504)

The irreverent Bastard immediately interjects, in what editors have often identified as an 'aside', meant to be heard by the audience but not the other characters, with a scathing critique of the Dauphin's metaphors:

> Drawn in the flattering table of her eye,
> Hanged in the frowning wrinkle of her brow,
> And quartered in her heart: he doth espy

> Himself love's traitor. This is pity now,
> That hanged and drawn and quartered there should be
> In such a love so vile a lout as he.
>
> (2.1.505–10)

The fact that the Bastard's critique is framed in the rhyme scheme of a sonnet sestet identifies the object of his satire as the sonnet discourse itself as well as the loutish, self-absorbed character who employs it.

The date of *King John* is still disputed, as is the date when Shakespeare's sonnets were written, but both are often dated in the mid-1590s. By that time—and certainly by the time the sonnets were finally published in 1609—the vogue of the Petrarchan sonnet must have seemed exhausted. In *Romeo and Juliet*, published twelve years earlier, its stale conventions had already provided the material for easy satire. At the beginning of the play, Romeo is depicted as a lovesick boy who uses conventional Petrarchan language to describe his infatuation with Rosaline. He begins with a rush of facile oxymorons: his love is a 'heavy lightness, serious vanity... feather of lead, bright smoke, cold fire, sick health', and 'waking sleep' (1.1.169–74). Conventionally hyperbolic, he describes his passion as 'a smoke made with the fume of sighs, | Being purged, a fire sparkling in lovers' eyes, | Being vexed, a sea nourished with lovers' tears' (1.1.182–5). He invokes the clichéd images of 'Cupid's arrow' and of courtship as 'the siege of loving terms' (1.1. 202, 205). Mercutio is not present during this scene, but when he wishes to deride Romeo's lovesickness, he turns immediately to the stereotypical figure of the Petrarchan sonneteer when he declares, 'Now is he for the numbers [i.e. verses] that Petrarch flowed in', and to a stereotypical Petrarchan trope when he imagines Romeo proclaiming that 'Laura to his lady was a kitchen wench—marry she had a better love to berhyme her' (2.3.34–6).

The date when *Romeo and Juliet* was first performed is not known, but it probably originated, along with most of the sonnets, in the mid-1590s. Certainly, the two texts are related to each other in numerous ways. In addition to a parodic version of the conventional imagery of previous sonneteers, the lovesick Romeo of Act I seems also to parody Shakespeare's own sonnets when he uses an argument against chastity very much like the one that Shakespeare himself uses in his first seventeen sonnets when he urges the fair youth to beget children in order to provide a lasting legacy of his beauty. Without children, these so-called 'procreation sonnets' charge, the young man is wasting the 'great...sum' of beauty bequeathed to him by nature, which will be 'tombed with [him]' when he dies (Sonnet 4). Romeo makes exactly the same argument when he complains that Rosaline, having sworn herself to chastity, 'is rich in beauty, only poor | That when she dies, with beauty dies her store' (1.1.208–9).

However, although Shakespeare's own practice as a sonneteer is not immune to satire in the context of the dramatic action in *Romeo and Juliet*, the sonnet tradition is also allowed to reassert its power. It is noteworthy that the language of the sonnets is not confined to Romeo's description of his infatuation with Rosaline. In fact, his very first conversation with Juliet takes the form of a sonnet (1.5.90–103). Just as Romeo and Juliet's story transforms the hyperbolic threats of the sonneteers to die for love into literal reality, the language Romeo and Juliet use to express their love transforms the tired lexicon of the sonnet tradition. Even their characteristic image of bright heavenly bodies shining in darkness recalls the formulaic paradoxes of the Petrarchan sonneteers. In fact, the entire play works by paradox and antithesis, from the paradoxical union of love and death that defines the lovers' passion to the opposed imagery of darkness and light in which they express it. In *Romeo and Juliet* Shakespeare not only satirized the hackneyed rhetorical strategy of an outworn poetic tradition; he also recuperated it to provide the basis for what has proved to be the most durable and convincing love poem ever written in the English language.

Like *Romeo and Juliet*, Shakespeare's sonnets stage a complicated negotiation with the Petrarchan tradition. Written at a time when the vogue of the sonnet sequence was so familiar that it was an easy subject for parody, even in plays written for the amusement of a public theatre audience, Shakespeare's sonnets were clearly belated. They were also novel, however, in two important respects. In the first place, their repeated subject is the speaker's devotion to a beautiful young man. Other poets, as far back as Dante and Petrarch, had written occasional sonnets of praise to male patrons and friends, but in Shakespeare's, the figure of the beautiful young man is assigned the central role traditionally occupied by the Petrarchan lady. Although many of Shakespeare's sonnets do not specify the gender of the beloved (and it is by no means certain that they were designed to be read in the order in which they were published in the first edition), it appears that the first 126 sonnets were addressed to one or more men. It is not clear whether these sonnets depict various stages or aspects of the speaker's relationship with a single man or express his feelings for a number of beloved persons, both male and female; but in many of these poems, a beautiful young man is endowed with the traditional attributes of the Petrarchan lady. His bright eyes are starlike, he himself resembles the sun, and he is also compared to flowers and other beautiful objects in nature. In temperament, he is often depicted as cold, remote, and unapproachable. He seems to occupy a social position higher than the poet's, and he is repeatedly represented as beloved rather than loving. Also like the Petrarchan lady, the fair young man is the inspiration for the poet's writing, which, in turn, will immortalize both the poet's voice and the beloved's image. In the later sonnets, when Shakespeare does introduce a lady, she is the complete opposite to the Petrarchan ideal. Dark rather than fair, she is also lustful rather than chaste; and instead of inspiring the poet to spiritual elevation, she degrades him in shameful lust.

Shakespeare's paired portraits of a beautiful, unattainable young man and a dark, promiscuous woman can easily be read as expressions of the deepest misogyny. But it is worth remembering that the Petrarchan tradition he challenged was also consistent with misogyny. Petrarch himself had written misogynist satires on women,[2] and the objectified, ideal lady of the Petrarchan sonnet tradition stood as an implicit rebuke to the human imperfection of women as they actually were. The Petrarchan lady modelled the features that constituted a beautiful woman—in life as well as in art. As Nancy Vickers has observed, 'Petrarch's figuration of Laura' played a crucial role 'in the development of a code of beauty... that causes us to view the fetishized body as a norm and encourages us to seek, or to seek to be, "ideal types, beautiful monsters composed of every individual perfection".'[3] In addition to discrediting the physical bodies of actual women, the Petrarchan ideal silenced women's voices. As Vickers observes, 'bodies fetishized by a poetic voice logically do not have a voice of their own' (p. 107). The poet's speech, in fact, requires the lady's silence (p. 109).

Shakespeare's dark lady is a notable exception, especially in Sonnet 130, which insists on the human imperfections of the lady's body, but uses them to discredit the Petrarchan ideal in terms that closely anticipate Vickers' critique.

> My mistress' eyes are nothing like the sun;
> Coral is far more red than her lips' red.
> If snow be white, why then her breasts are dun;
> If hairs be wires, black wires grow on her head.
> I have seen roses damasked, red and white,
> But no such roses see I in her cheeks;
> And in some perfumes is there more delight
> Than in the breath that from my mistress reeks.
> I love to hear her speak, yet well I know
> That music hath a far more pleasing sound.
> I grant I never saw a goddess go:
> My mistress when she walks treads on the ground.
>> And yet, by heaven, I think my love as rare
>> As any she belied with false compare.

This sonnet constitutes a remarkable anomaly, not only among the sonnets that surround it in Shakespeare's own collection but also within the larger tradition of Petrarchan sonnets with which it engages. To be sure, this is not the only sonnet in which Shakespeare repudiates the conventions of Petrarchan praise. In Sonnet 21, for instance, apparently addressed to the young man, he dismisses the tradition of comparing the beloved 'with sun and moon, with earth, and sea's rich gems, | With April's first-born flowers, and all things rare'. Instead, he writes,

> O let me, true in love, but truly write,
> And then believe me my love is as fair
> As any mother's child, though not so bright
> As those gold candles [i.e. the stars] fixed in heaven's air.
> Let them say more that like of hearsay well;
> I will not praise that purpose not to sell.

Here, as in Sonnet 130, Shakespeare rejects the hyperbolic conventions of Petrarchan comparison in order to claim sincerity for his own love. What is different about 130 is the detailed specificity of both the rejection of the Petrarchan conventions and the description of the beloved person.

Describing a woman with dun-coloured breasts, whose hair resembles black wires growing on her head and whose breath reeks with an all-too-human odour, Sonnet 130 is remarkably graphic in its repudiation of the Petrarchan ideal. The repellent details of the woman's description in this sonnet confront its readers with the unspoken shadow of the Petrarchan lady, who is here identified as an impossible ideal, constructed as an aggregate of inhuman similes that deny the reality of women's bodies and the sexual disgust they could evoke. Older criticism typically resisted that confrontation, sanitizing the woman's description in Sonnet 130 as 'playful' and emphasizing that at the time this sonnet was written, 'reeks' need not have meant 'stinks'.

Modern editors have spent more time glossing 'reeks' than any other word in the poem, attempting to neutralize its nasty connotations by carefully explaining that it had not yet acquired its current pejorative meaning. Douglas Bush and Alfred Harbage, in their 1961 Pelican edition, glossed 'reeks' as 'breathes forth'. A 1964 casebook on the sonnets flatly declares, 'The modern sense of "smell unpleasant" was not used in Elizabethan English'.[4] *The Riverside Shakespeare* was careful to inform its readers that 'reeks' meant 'is exhaled (without pejorative connotation)'. Even so astute a critic as Stephen Orgel notes in his 2001 Penguin edition that 'reeks' was 'not pejorative until the eighteenth century'. These glosses are misleading because, although the pejorative connotations were not yet as firmly attached to the word as they have since become, they were already there—and had been for several hundred years. As early as 1430, John Lydgate had used 'reek' to describe the odour of sweat, and both Shakespeare and his contemporaries had also used it to describe unpleasant odours, such as blood and sweat, including the sweat of a horse. One sixteenth-century writer explicitly used the word as a synonym for 'stink'.[5] Shakespeare himself used it in *Henry V* to describe the odour of dead bodies buried in dunghills (4.4.102). In the face of all this lexical evidence—easily obtainable, since it is cited in the *Oxford English Dictionary*—the scholarly reluctance to accept even the possibility that the poet found the lady's breath disagreeable seems more than merely fastidious. The shameful secret is not simply that the lady may have had bad breath. It is the disgust for the flesh—especially female flesh—that would prevent the poet from loving (or the scholar from imagining him loving) a lady who smelled like anything less delightful (or more human) than perfume.

The sexual loathing that shadowed the Petrarchan ideal had a long and venerable genealogy in medieval Christian contempt for the flesh, and for female flesh in particular. In medieval thought, all flesh, male as well as female, tended to fall on the wrong side of the binary opposition that divided masculine from feminine gender. A woman, said St Jerome, is 'different from man as body is from soul'.[6] These associations did not disappear with the Reformation.[7] To Martin Luther, 'we are the woman because of the flesh, that is, we are carnal, and we are the man because of the spirit . . . we are at the same time both dead and set free'. This same distinction between masculine spirit and feminine flesh can be seen as late as the middle of the seventeenth century, when the radical reformer Gerrard Winstanley condemned sinners who had 'been led by the powers of the curse in flesh, which is the *Feminine* part; not by the power of the righteous Spirit which is Christ, the *Masculine* power'.[8] The images that define the difference between the speaker's two loves in Sonnet 144 draw explicitly on this misogynist tradition. The speaker, like the protagonist of a Christian morality play, is pulled between two figures. His 'better angel', a 'saint', is 'a man right fair'. His 'worser spirit' is 'a woman coloured ill', a 'female evil', who threatens to separate the speaker from his good angel by corrupting the young man, wooing his 'purity' with her 'foul pride' (a word that conflates lust with the worst of the seven deadly sins). The speaker imagines the young man in the woman's 'hell', a metaphor that identifies the site of damnation with her vagina.

Although indebted to Christian misogyny, the gendering of lust as female was also ratified by classical tradition, which allowed for a spiritual love between man and man but not between man and woman. A reference to this tradition in a text roughly contemporary with Shakespeare's sonnets appeared in Edmund Spenser's *Shepheardes Calender* (1579), a set of twelve pastoral eclogues, which were published with marginal 'glosses', or comments, attributed to a writer identified as 'E.K.'. In a gloss to the January eclogue, E.K. invokes classical precedent to argue that '*paederastice* is much to be preferred before *gynerastice*' because unlike 'the love which enflameth men with lust toward woman kind', male homoerotic love could be purely spiritual. He offers the example of Socrates' love for Alcibiades, whose object, he argues, was not the young man's 'person, but hys soule, which is Alcybiades owne selfe'.

The unease provoked by the story of homoerotic desire that seems to lie behind Shakespeare's sonnets appears to be a distinctly post-Shakespearian phenomenon. In Shakespeare's own time, as Margreta de Grazia has persuasively argued, the true 'scandal of Shakespeare's sonnets' was undoubtedly his lustful passion for the dark lady. That passion, unlike his love for the young man, cannot be sublimated because it represents a threat to the genealogically and racially based social distinctions that are celebrated in the sonnets addressed to the fair, aristocratic young man. 'The bay where all men ride' (Sonnet 137), the woman's body is a place of pollution that threatens to mingle aristocratic with common and black with fair blood.[9] The furious misogyny of the dark lady sonnets is authorized by a long tradition of medieval and Renaissance thought that defined a man's sexual passion for a woman as dangerous and degrading, but it is also fuelled by the biological capacity of the dark, promiscuous woman to produce mongrel children.

That fury is probably most explicit in Sonnet 129, which characterizes sexual congress as an 'expense of spirit in a waste of shame', and sexual desire as a poisoned bait which drives 'the taker mad' and 'leads men to this hell'. As Thomas Greene notes, this sonnet expresses a view of sexual intercourse which, while strikingly different from 'the restorative, therapeutic release our post-Freudian society perceives', was commonly accepted in Shakespeare's time.[10] As Greene also points out, the sonnet draws on the medieval and Renaissance belief that sexual intercourse shortened a man's life. But it is also noteworthy that the sonnet genders the passion it condemns as heterosexual and identifies the danger it threatens as a danger to men. Here, as in Sonnet 144, the word 'hell' conflates the woman's vagina with the place of eternal damnation and torment. Moreover, the lust the sonnet condemns was identified as a feminine and effeminating vice. It was not until the end of the nineteenth century, with the Oscar Wilde trials, that male effeminacy was identified with homosexual desire.[11] In the Middle Ages and Renaissance, although excessive passion in either sex was condemned, women were believed to be more lustful than men: sculptured images of the deadly sins that adorned medieval cathedrals depicted lust as a woman, and excessive lust in men was regarded as a mark of effeminacy. In Shakespeare's sonnets, the speaker's lust for the woman reduces him to the level of an animal who swallows a poisoned bait; swallowed, the bait drives him mad, his higher reason overcome by his base bodily appetites. It also renders him effeminate because manliness required rational self-control.

Critical uneasiness about the homoerotic passion expressed in the sonnets is based on the modern belief that the dividing line between virility and effeminacy is based on sexual orientation: virile men desire women; effeminate men desire other men. This uneasiness has produced arguments either that the sonnets have nothing to tell us about Shakespeare's personal feelings or that the love they express, although Shakespeare's, is not actually homoerotic (de Grazia, p. 40). However, the passion that is identified as effeminating in Shakespeare's sonnets is not his homoerotic love for the young man but rather his heterosexual lust for the dark lady; and the critics have been equally evasive in their discussions of the dark lady sonnets. The story of the poet's degrading lust for a sexually promiscuous dark woman is typically read as a witty rebuttal to the Petrarchan idealization of fair, unattainable ladies and the ennobling effects of loving them. As far as they go, these readings are generally convincing, but they insulate the misogyny expressed in most of the dark lady sonnets within the sanitized precincts of literary history. The hysterical misogyny those sonnets express is rarely acknowledged, either as Shakespeare's own pathology or as the dark underside of the Petrarchan tradition itself.

The remarkable power of the misogynist sonnets is no guarantee, of course, that they contain autobiographical revelations. Shakespeare's plays provide overwhelming evidence that he was capable of expressing virtually any sentiment with a thoroughly convincing eloquence. These sonnets may equally well have been written to cater to the taste of an aristocratic patron or that of the readers Shakespeare hoped to impress. But regardless of their autobiographical import, they constitute a powerful register of the pathological misogyny that coexisted with Petrarchan idealization and, indeed, constituted the foul matrix in which it grew. If women's lust was dangerous to men, the Petrarchan lady had to be icily chaste. If women's bestial, corporeal bodies were inherently loathsome, the Petrarchan lady had to be compounded of sweet flowers, precious jewels, and bright, remote heavenly bodies. What matters in those sonnets is not Shakespeare's personal feelings, which remain unknowable, but their contribution to a misogynist legacy that persists even in the twenty-first century, in the advertisements for a flourishing cosmetics industry, in the epidemic of anorexia as teenaged girls starve their developing bodies, and in the agonies of self-loathing that drive mature women to endure the painful mutilations of liposuction and plastic surgery.

In view of that legacy, Sonnet 130 deserves much closer attention than it has usually received, for it offers a direct challenge to its readers to confront and disown the paradoxical union of misogyny and sublimation that produced the Petrarchan ideal. What makes this sonnet so remarkable is that it claims as an object of love a lady who is not sanitized by Petrarchan abstraction, idealization, and dismembered commodification. Scholarly commentators, however, have typically warned their readers against taking Sonnet 130 too seriously. Stephen Booth wrote, 'This poem, a winsome trifle is easily distorted into a solemn critical statement about sonnet conventions.'[12] Murray Krieger was fascinated by the ways Shakespeare's sonnets 'wrestled' with the Petrarchan convention, but he dismissed Sonnet 130 as a 'too obvious' 'example of anti-Petrarchan Petrarchism' and merely 'playful'.[13]

These dismissive judgements would be accurate if the poem ended after the first quatrain, which reads like a simply reversed version of a Petrarchan catalogue poem, differing only in that each of the conventional comparisons is denied. As in a typical catalogue sonnet, one line each is given to eyes, lips, breast, and hair, listed in no apparent order, simply as an itemized list. The Petrarchan catalogue also formed the subject of easy parody in *Twelfth Night* in an interchange that emphasizes the artificiality of sonneteering rhetoric. Viola, disguised as the boy Cesario, has been sent to court Olivia on behalf of her master. Reciting what she says is a 'part' she has 'studied' (1.5. 158–9), she presents Olivia with an abbreviated version of the same argument against celibacy that Shakespeare had used in his own sonnets (and also as an object of mockery in *Romeo and Juliet*). Viola declares, in hyperbolic verse,

> Lady, you are the cruell'st she alive
> If you will lead these graces to the grave
> And leave the world no copy.
>
> (1.5.211–13)

Olivia's response is prosaic and matter-of-fact, deflating the hyperbolic conceit by offering to leave a will accompanied by another kind of copy, an inventoried list of her features:

O sir, I will not be so hard-hearted. I will give out divers schedules of my beauty. It shall be inventoried and every particle and utensil labelled to my will, as, *item*, two lips, indifferent red; *item*, two grey eyes, with lids to them; *item*, one neck, one chin, and so forth. (1.5.214–18)

In Sonnet 130, the lover uses a similar literalism to deflate the hyperbolic terms of Petrarchan praise, listing in what looks at first like a random inventory a collection of conventional Petrarchan comparisons, each of which is invoked only to be denied. By the end of the poem, however, it is clear that it is not the lady but the comparisons themselves that he finds inadequate. Moreover, the stakes in Sonnet 130 are considerably higher than they are in the easy satire of Petrarchan convention that was itself a commonplace by the time this sonnet was written. This anti-Petrarchan critique is far more searching, and the final turn to a declaration of love is much harder won. What begins in Sonnet 130 as an apparently random list of discrete attributes ends by evoking the presence of a living woman. Even as he admits that the lady's breath does not smell like perfume, that her voice is far less pleasing than music, and that he cannot compare her gait to that of a goddess, the poet reminds us that she breathes and speaks, that she walks, and that the object of his love is a real woman, alive and active.

The transformation begins in the second quatrain. After the rapidly itemized inventory of eyes, lips, breast, and hair, the second quatrain slows down, devoting two lines each to cheeks and breath; and it moves purposefully from the colour of the lady's cheeks to the scent of her breath. The terms of the description proceed from the detached, evaluative sense of sight to the intimacy of scent. At the same time, with the mention of her breath, the lady herself comes to life. The attributes described in the first six lines—lips less red than coral, dun-coloured breasts, hairs like black wires, cheeks that do not resemble damask roses—could just as easily belong to an effigy or a corpse. In their descriptions, moreover, there is no indication that the speaker regards the lady with anything but disdain. It is not until the beginning of the third quatrain that he reveals, 'I love to hear her speak'.

Significantly, that revelation comes immediately following the reference to the lady's breath—a reference that has often seemed to be the most damaging description of all. But the lady's reeking breath marks the turning point in the sonnet's action. The first attribute named that can belong only to a living creature, it both incorporates and radically revises the traditional Christian association of breath with spirit, the principle of life that emanated from God; for although the reference to the lady's reeking breath calls her to life, the life it evokes is overwhelmingly physical. As such, it directly challenges a crucial element of the sonnet tradition, which was informed from the time of Petrarch with the traditional Platonic and Christian ascetic dualism that privileged divine spirit over earthly matter. The reference to the lady's reeking breath initiates a celebration of her flesh, living, but neither sublimated nor sanitized.

It is also significant that the lady's breath is the first attribute named that cannot be detected by sight, the most judgemental of the senses and the most physically and emotionally detached. In moving from the lady's eyes to her breath and from the poet's sight to his other senses, the poem inverts not only the hierarchy of matter and spirit, but also the related hierarchy of the senses, both of which were widely accepted in Renaissance thought. Building on the arguments in Plato's *Republic* and *Timaeus* and Aristotle's *Metaphysics*, medieval and Renaissance thinkers understood the senses to be ranged in a hierarchical order with sight, associated with reason and God, as the highest, followed by hearing and the lower senses of smell, taste, and touch. The opening line of the sonnet—'My mistress' eyes are nothing like the sun'—reads like a direct answer to Plato's argument that sight is the highest of the senses because 'of all the organs of sense the eye is the most like the sun'.[14] Rejecting the Platonic comparison, the sonnet also inverts the Platonic hierarchy of the senses, for it is only after the speaker abandons the detached, comparative judgements of sight for the intimate, earth-bound sense of smell that he can begin to speak of the attributes that make his mistress beloved.

The Shakespearian sonnet, unlike the Petrarchan, is characteristic-ally divided by its rhyme scheme into three quatrains and a couplet rather than an octave and a sestet; but in many of Shakespeare's sonnets, there is a conceptual break between the second and third quatrains, which remembers the old division. In Sonnet 130, the second quatrain ends with the description of the lady's breath, the first attribute that cannot be detected by sight, and the first that could only belong to a living woman; and the third quatrain begins with the first revelation of the speaker's true feelings—'I love to hear her speak'. The third quatrain also continues and intensifies the recon-stitution of the lady as a living woman. In the first eight lines, every item in the description—even the lady's breath—was a discrete, static entity, designated by a noun. In the third quatrain, verbs replace nouns as the lady speaks and walks. No longer a lifeless collection of inert, disjointed attributes, the lady has come to life as an active human presence. The breath of life initiated the transformation; what completes it are her speaking voice and her solid, earthbound corpor-eality as she 'treads on the ground'.

Although Sonnet 130 seems to anticipate modern feminist critiques that identify the inherent misogyny of the Petrarchan tradition, there is no doubt that Shakespeare was also capable of imagining, and perhaps also feeling, the most pathological extremes of sexual loathing. One has only to think of Lear's furious denunciations of female flesh:

> The fitchew [i.e. polecat] nor the soiléd horse, goes to't
> With a more riotous appetite.
> Down from the waist they are Centaurs,
> Though women all above.
> But to the girdle do the gods inherit.
> Beneath is all the fiends'; there's hell, there's darkness,
> There's the sulphurous pit, burning, scalding,
> Stench, consumption! Fie, fie, fie! pah! pah!
> Give me an ounce of civet, good apothecary,
> To sweeten my imagination.
>   (Conflated Text, 4.6.119–28)

Lear is mad when he speaks these lines, as a result of his daughters' betrayal, but although this is a particularly vivid example, many characters, both in *King Lear* and in other plays, express similar sentiments. A similar vocabulary of moral condemnation and sexual loathing appears repeatedly in the sonnets addressed to the dark lady: she is 'foul', a 'devil', or a 'fiend'. The repeated metaphor for her genitalia is 'hell'. Clearly, the sentiments expressed in Sonnet 130 are strikingly atypical, not only within the larger Petrarchan tradition, but also within Shakespeare's own oeuvre. They do not, therefore, provide any basis for claiming Shakespeare as a feminist *avant la lettre*.

The most plausible explanation for Sonnet 130 is that it is a poetic *tour de force*. Written at a time when the Petrarchan tradition was all but exhausted, it offers a profound criticism of the traditional tropes of Petrarchan praise, but manages even as it does so to accomplish exactly what those tropes were designed to achieve; for the essential project of Petrarchan poetry was not simply or even primarily to celebrate the beloved lady but to display the poet's virtuosity in competition with his long line of predecessors in the tradition. However, the originality and intellectual rigour with which Sonnet 130 challenges that tradition and imagines a love whose object is an actual woman rather than a disembodied ideal opens a place within the misogynist corpus of Petrarchan poetry in which real women can imagine themselves as the objects of a heterosexual love that is not tainted by the misogynist disgust that elsewhere shadows the Petrarchan ideal.

Many of Shakespeare's sonnets, of course, give powerful expression to that disgust. Sonnet 130 is an anomaly not only within the sonnet tradition but also within the corpus of Shakespeare's own sonnets. It is important, not because it tells us anything about Shakespeare's true feelings, but because of what it enables its readers to imagine. The temptation to scrutinize Shakespeare's writings for evidence of his personal commitments remains tantalizing, even though it has been repeatedly discredited. But if the pursuit of autobiographical revelations is doomed to disappointment—and I believe it is—the desire that animates that pursuit is not. Far from a disinterested scholarly curiosity about Shakespeare's feelings and motivations, the impulse that makes that pursuit so tantalizing is a very interested desire to claim Shakespeare's authority for whatever one's own beliefs and opinions happen to be. Thus, Shakespeare has been claimed as, *inter alia*, a royalist, a democrat, a Catholic, a Puritan, a protofeminist, and a misogynist. All of these claims, and many others, have been strenuously argued and documented with abundant quotations from his writings and just as strenuously refuted. What is indisputable, however, is that he was a writer of remarkable power and that his writing still has an authority unequalled by any other secular texts. For women, therefore, what matters is not what Shakespeare thought and felt about us, but what the words he wrote enable us to think and feel about ourselves.

Shakespeare's Timeless Women

The female characters we encounter in Shakespeare's plays are not the same ones that appeared in the original productions. In the theatre, we rarely see them portrayed by male actors, but even in reading the women we imagine represent the end product of over four hundred years of modernization to redefine their roles in terms of new conceptions of women's nature and women's roles in the world. Not all of Shakespeare's women have changed to the same degree: in some cases they have been easily recruited to serve as role models—both positive and negative—for women born hundreds of years after their original creation. In other cases, they have required more updating because the fit between the roles they originally had and the roles post-Shakespearian readers and revisers have imagined for them is less than seamless. An examination of the roles that have been most drastically reshaped both in theatrical production and in readers' comments can tell us a great deal about the history of women's roles in the disparate worlds in which the plays have been performed and read. Paradoxically, however, this implication of Shakespeare's female characters in the process of historical change has tended to occlude their own historicity, as they served, and continue to serve, in ever-changing guises as models of an unchanging, universal female nature.

It is also important to recognize that this process of updating Shakespeare's female characters and the consequent occlusion of their historical difference did not begin with post-Shakespearian revisers. Shakespeare himself often updated the women he found in his historical sources to shape their roles in forms that made them recognizable in terms of his own contemporaries' expectations about

2. Charlotte Cushman as Lady Macbeth (1858)

women's behaviour and motivation. These changes offer a revealing glimpse of the contested and changing gender ideology that shaped Shakespeare's original audiences' conceptions of women's proper roles, not only in the plays they went to see but also in the lives they lived.

Probably the most obvious manifestation of the way the updating of Shakespeare's female characters both bespeaks and obscures their historical location can be seen in theatrical costume. Illustrations of eighteenth- and nineteenth- and even early twentieth-century productions of the plays almost always look outdated. In their own time, the costumes and sets these illustrations depict were undoubtedly designed to provide the most appropriate possible realizations of the characters Shakespeare created, but in ours they look like quaint period pieces, and the period to which they belong is not that in which the plays were originally set or produced but that of their own production (see Figure 2). Clearly, what these illustrations show us is not the way the characters were originally conceived but the ways they were imagined in times and places that are now unmistakably marked as distant, both from our own world and from that of Shakespeare. Illustrations of recent productions, by contrast, tend to obscure their own historicity, coming to us either as 'authentic' recreations of the plays' original productions or their historical settings, or else as manifestations of the timeless contemporaneity of Shakespeare's representations of universal human experience.

The only sixteenth-century illustration of a Shakespearian text that we have is a drawing that dates from the mid-1590s in which Tamora, the Queen of the Goths in *Titus Andronicus*, pleads with Titus to spare her two sons. In keeping with the ancient Roman setting of the play, Titus is dressed in a classical-looking draped garment, perhaps copied from a Roman statue; but Tamora wears a much more modern costume (see Figure 3). We do not have an illustration of Cleopatra as she appeared when *Antony and Cleopatra* was first performed, but the playscript indicates that too she must have been dressed in anachronistically modern clothing. Early in the play (1.3.71), Shakespeare's ancient Egyptian queen orders her attendant to cut her lace, a demand that would have made sense only if she wore a tight, stiffened busk or bodice like the costumes worn by fashionable ladies in Shakespeare's own time. To be sure, on Shakespeare's stage modern costume was more the rule than the exception: the two soldiers who attend Titus are

3. Characters from *Titus Andronicus* (*c.*1595)

also dressed in contemporary Elizabethan costume; in *Julius Caesar,* the conspirators pluck anachronistic hats about their ears (2.1.63); in *Richard II,* one courtier threatens another with an anachronistic rapier (4.1.39); and many other examples could be cited. Nonetheless, the anachronism of Tamora's costume is suggestive because it implies that even when her male antagonist is seen as belonging to a specific historical context, the woman's characterization is untouched by the contingencies of time and place.

The anachronism that erases the historicity of the woman and the plebeian men in the illustration from *Titus Andronicus* lies deeper than dress. Here, as in Shakespeare's English history plays, historical location seems to be a privilege reserved for royal and aristocratic men. The Henry IV plays, which cover a broad spectrum of society, provide a striking example. The king's court, inhabited exclusively by high-born men, is relatively free of anachronisms, and of women as well. Not even the queen appears. The Eastcheap tavern, by contrast, is presided over by a woman, Mistress Quickly, and it is depicted in strikingly contemporary terms. Mistress Quickly entertains a dissolute crew of lowlife men with anachronistic cups of sack, a wine that was not served in English taverns until 1543.[1] She is accompanied by another woman, the prostitute Doll Tearsheet, who reproaches the anachronistically named Pistol for tearing her anachronistically Elizabethan ruff (*2 Henry IV*: 2.4.113–20).

Mistress Quickly and Doll, like the low-life men they entertain, are placed in an anachronistically contemporary setting that separates them from the high-born men at the king's historical court. But in the case of the women, their anachronistic location is overdetermined because in these plays, even the high-born women are conceived in anachronistic terms. Hotspur's wife, unlike Doll and the Hostess, had a real historical prototype—the granddaughter of Lionel, Duke of Clarence, the same ancestor on whom the Mortimers based their claim to the English throne—but she too seems to inhabit the present world of Shakespeare's audience rather than the late fourteenth-century world of her historical prototype. Hotspur claims that she swears 'like a comfit-maker's wife' (3.1.243–4)

> And giv'st such sarcenet surety for thy oaths
> As if thou never walk'st further than Finsbury.
> Swear me, Kate, like a lady as thou art,
> A good mouth-filling oath, and leave 'in sooth'
> And such protest of pepper gingerbread
> To velvet-guards and Sunday citizens.
>
> (*1 Henry IV*: 3.1.247–52)

All these details—the references to confectioners and their wares; to Finsbury, a district of open walks and fields favoured by London citizens; to the velvet guards that ornamented the gowns of aldermen's wives—associate Shakespeare's Lady Percy with the late sixteenth-century citizens' wives in his playhouse, even though her historical prototype had died in 1403. The anachronistic details of speech and dress evoke a contemporary female stereotype—that of the respectable citizen's wife—which would have been entirely familiar to members of Shakespeare's original audience. Hotspur's speech must have been good for a laugh in a sixteenth-century playhouse, probably at the expense of women who were actually present in the audience, but the topical details that made it funny rest on an assumption with totally serious implications. Like Tamora's anachronistic costume and Cleopatra's anachronistic laces, they depend on— and also reinforce—the assumption that women are always and everywhere the same, immune to the historical contingencies of time and place. They interpellate the women in the audience with identities that are defined solely by their gender—identities constrained by usually hostile and always restrictive stereotypes.

Of all Shakespeare's female characters, the figure who seems to offer the most unmanageable resistance to those stereotypes is Cleopatra. It is not surprising that modern film-makers have never chosen to produce Shakespeare's version of her story as a big-budget film, despite the obvious attractions of the fabulous Egyptian queen as a cinematic subject.[2] Already legendary when Shakespeare produced his version of her story, the powerfully ambivalent Cleopatra he staged drew on a variety of sources. These included the Roman writers who had defined her as the Eastern, barbarian, 'harlot queen' and the fifteenth- and sixteenth-century predecessors who had identified her with the threatening power of women's insatiable appetite[3] as well as the antitheatrical polemicists who had insisted on the deceptiveness and corruption of Shakespeare's own theatrical medium. The combination of erotic power and political authority that had made Cleopatra such a troubling figure to Romans and humanists alike might also have struck a responsive chord in Shakespeare's original audiences: they had, until very recently, lived under the sway of their own powerful queen. For twentieth-century American filmgoers, by contrast, Cleopatra had to be reduced to a fetishized

4. Elizabeth Taylor as Cleopatra (1963), Photofest, New York

female body, adorned in spectacular costumes for the pleasure of male spectators and the emulation of other women (see Figure 4). Her motivation is clear and simple: to please her man. In the 1963 Joseph Mankiewicz film, for instance, Cleopatra's suicide is no longer staged as a demonstration of her royalty. Instead of ordering her women to 'show me ... like a queen', Elizabeth Taylor's Cleopatra says, 'I will wear—I want to be as Antony first saw me. He must know at once, and from a great distance, that it is I.' As Katherine Eggert observes, the film 'domesticates Cleopatra into a spectacular mannequin who intends to give pleasure only to her man' (p. 205).

Even at the end of the seventeenth century, when John Dryden produced his own version of the play, he found it necessary to transform Shakespeare's dangerously powerful and supremely artful heroine into a stereotype of artless feminine helplessness. The Cleopatra of Dryden's *All for Love* (1678) explicitly declares,

> Nature meant me
> A wife, a silly, harmless household dove,
> Fond without art, and kind without deceit;
> But Fortune, that has made a mistress of me,
> Has thrust me out to the wide world, unfurnished
> Of falsehood to be happy.
>
> (4.1.91–6)

There is no indication in Dryden's script that he intended these lines as anything more than a sincere expression of his heroine's perfectly womanly nature. His play supplanted Shakespeare's throughout the Restoration and eighteenth century.[4] As such, it participated in the codification of the gendered morality of private life that was to be a central tenet of modern Western belief.

Dryden's play, unlike Shakespeare's, brings Octavia to Alexandria for a meeting with Cleopatra, an encounter that Dryden justifies in his Preface as a 'natural' expression of their characters as women:

I judged it both natural and probable that Octavia, proud of her new-gained conquest, would search out Cleopatra to triumph over her, and that Cleopatra, thus attacked, was not of a spirit to shun the encounter; and 'tis not unlikely that two exasperated rivals should use such satire as I have put into their mouths, for, after all, though the one was a Roman and the other a queen, they were both women.[5]

To justify his innovation, Dryden relies on what he imagines as the unchanging 'nature' of women to discount any distinctions of nationality, rank, or historicity.

Dryden wrote at a time when neoclassical beliefs that general nature should supersede the accidents of individual identity in the representation of dramatic characters were widely endorsed; and *All for Love* was explicitly designed as a new version of the story of Antony and Cleopatra rather than merely an adaptation of Shakespeare's play. Nonetheless, Dryden's insistence upon transforming Shakespeare's female characters to bring them into conformity with what he regarded as an unchanging female nature outlasted his era. Even when Shakespeare's plays were not rewritten, the women's roles were repeatedly reshaped to fit the Procrustean bed of whatever gender ideology prevailed at the time and place of the play's production. This practice is strikingly illustrated in the collection of nineteenth-century images of Shakespeare's heroines that were exhibited in 1997 at the Folger Shakespeare Library in Washington, DC. As Georgianna Ziegler pointed out in the accompanying catalogue, Shakespeare's female characters were imagined to conform to Victorian ideals of female behaviour. She notes that even Lady Macbeth was redeemed as a good, Victorian wife, a woman whose 'ambition was all for her husband'.[6]

If, as Ziegler argues, 'Lady Macbeth, with her aggressiveness and murderous instincts turned to madness, was one of the most difficult of Shakespeare's heroines for the nineteenth century to appropriate' (p. 73), she has proved remarkably adaptable to twentieth-century understandings of feminine psychology. To Mary McCarthy, writing in the early 1960s, Lady Macbeth was clearly recognizable in contemporary terms as

a woman and has 'unsexed' herself, which makes her a monster by definition . . . the very prospect of murder quickens an hysterical excitement in her, like the discovery of some object in a shop—a set of emeralds or a sable stole—which Macbeth can give her and which will be an 'outlet' for all the repressed desires he cannot satisfy. She behaves as though Macbeth, through his weakness, will deprive her of self-realization; the unimpeded exercise of her will is the voluptuous end she seeks.

McCarthy's references to 'hysteria', repressed and unsatisfied desires that are clearly sexual, and a lust for the glittering objects of conspicuous consumption mark her diatribe as a mid-twentieth-century period piece; but it, no less than the Victorian *apologia* cited by Ziegler, measures the character against modern norms of wifely behaviour. 'Her wifely concern', McCarthy charges, 'is mechanical and far from real solicitude'. She regards her husband 'as a thing, a tool that must be oiled and polished'.[7] Despite the three centuries that separated Dryden's Cleopatra from the Victorians' and Mary McCarthy's Lady Macbeth, and despite the manifold differences between the roles of the two characters and the playworlds in which Shakespeare set them, all were judged by reference to the paradigmatic modern embodiment of female virtue, the good wife. Dryden's Cleopatra may have been engaged in an illicit alliance with Antony, but—like all good women—she was designed by nature for marriage and domesticity as a 'wife, a silly, harmless household dove'. The Victorians' Lady Macbeth may have been guilty of regicide, but, like all good women, she was motivated by ambition for her husband's advancement. Mary McCarthy's Lady Macbeth was monstrously unwomanly because she was ambitious only for herself.

McCarthy's satirical portrait of Lady Macbeth is exaggerated and oversimplified, but it expresses in the simplest possible terms the preoccupations with her sexuality and her relationship with her husband that have dominated modern conceptions of her character. Modern critics and playgoers, like McCarthy, have found in Lady Macbeth a character easily understandable in terms of their own preconceptions about female psychology, especially in the soliloquy in which Lady Macbeth calls on murderous spirits to 'unsex' her (1.5.36–52). Along with the sleepwalking scene, this soliloquy offers a great showpiece for modern actresses, as well as a powerful advertisement for modern assumptions about female character. Often accompanied by autoerotic display as the actress fondles her own breasts, breathes hard, and writhes in the throes of passion, the speech clearly demonstrates that the lady is, in fact, sexed; and it locates her sex in the eroticized breasts of the woman who performs the role. On a modern stage, its meaning seems perfectly transparent.

The implications of the speech when it was first performed would have been much more complicated. First, of course, it would have been spoken by a male actor. Some scholars have speculated that the actor may have gestured toward his crotch when he said 'unsex me here', alluding to his own 'unsexing' as he took on the woman's part. However, although it is impossible to know exactly how the soliloquy was originally performed, the references in the speech to 'my woman's breasts' and 'my milk' suggest that he probably did gesture towards the place where the woman's breasts would have been if he had them. But although the erotic implications of the character's breasts seem overwhelming in a modern production, they may have been much less central on Shakespeare's stage, not only because the original actor did not really have a woman's breasts but also because women's breasts had other implications as well as the erotic. To modern Western eyes, the eroticization of women's breasts seems 'natural'; on a modern stage, the meaning of Lady Macbeth's soliloquy seems equally self-evident. The beliefs it assumes—that there is a psychological polarity between men and women, based on sexual differences that are embodied, natural, biologically grounded, and visually self-evident—are by now too familiar to require explication. At the time the speech was written, however, these assumptions did not yet represent a cultural consensus. In the Renaissance, although women's breasts were already eroticized as tokens of female sexuality, celebrated by poets as 'buds', 'strawberries', or 'hemispheres', and featured in erotic paintings that depicted women with a man's proprietary hand cupped on their breasts,[8] this was not their only implication, and it may not have even been their primary one. Medieval images of the lactating Virgin, of the Church allegorized as a nursing mother, and of souls suckled at the breast of Christ, which associated breast milk with charity and spiritual sustenance,[9] were still current in the Renaissance and still powerful; and they resonate in the details of the soliloquy Shakespeare wrote.

That soliloquy, spoken by Lady Macbeth in order to steel herself for Duncan's murder, is worth quoting at length. She calls on the 'spirits | That tend on mortal thoughts' to

> unsex me here,
> And fill me from the crown to the toe top-full
> Of direst cruelty. Make thick my blood,
> Stop up th' access and passage to remorse,
> That no compunctious visitings of nature
> Shake my fell purpose, nor keep peace between
> Th' effect and it. Come to my woman's breasts,
> And take my milk for gall, you murd'ring ministers,
> Wherever in your sightless substances
> You wait on nature's mischief. Come, thick night,
> And pall thee in the dunnest smoke of hell,
> That my keen knife see not the wound it makes,
> Nor heaven peep through the blanket of the dark
> To cry 'Hold, hold!'
>
> (1.5.38–52)

The 'smoke of hell' locates Lady Macbeth's desires in a theological context, as does her reference to remorse and compunction. Her supplication to 'take my milk for gall' suggests a diabolical exchange, in which she will exchange those benevolent feelings for the poisonous bitterness that will enable her to murder Duncan; and it also carries the suggestion that she is inviting the evil spirits she is invoking to feed on her, as witches were believed to feed the demonic imps who served as their 'familiars'. This is not the only context, of course. Lady Macbeth's association of her woman's milk with remorse and compunction also implies that women have a natural aversion to killing, physically grounded in their sexed and gendered bodies, which are designed to feed and nurture. Before she can kill, the spirits that 'wait on nature's mischief' will have to 'unsex' her.

This implication that feminine gentleness is grounded by nature in a lactating female body is clearly legible in twenty-first-century terms. It also provides a striking example of the ways Shakespeare's female characters have participated in the historical production of femininity as naturally grounded in women's roles as wives and mothers, not because it misreads Shakespeare's playscript, but because it does not. In this speech, Shakespeare transformed his historical sources to define Lady Macbeth's character in terms of an emergent gender ideology that culminated, over three centuries later, in the kind of reading I quoted from Mary McCarthy. The beginnings of the process can be seen in Shakespeare's transformations of his character's historical prototype, and post-Shakespearian transformations of the character he created illustrate its realization, especially in twentieth-century readings which emphasize her sexuality and analyse her behaviour in psychoanalytic terms. But the version of Lady Macbeth that looks so familiar to modern audiences is the product of a long history of anachronistic revision, not only because the psychological motivation we so easily recognize is distinctly modern but also because Shakespeare's own representation of her character required a radical revision of the descriptions of ancient Scotswomen he found in his historical source.

As M. C. Bradbrook pointed out over forty years ago, Lady Macbeth's soliloquy should probably be read in connection with a passage in Holinshed's *Chronicles* in a chapter entitled 'Of the Manners of the Scots in these Days, and their Comparison with the

Behaviour of the Old, and Such as Lived Long Since within this Island'.[10] As the title suggests, the chapter's theme is the conventional Renaissance opposition between a virile, heroic past and a degenerate, effeminate present. In ancient Scotland, according to the chronicler,

the women ... were of no less courage than the men; for all stout maidens and wives ... marched as well in the field as did the men, and so soon as the army did set forward, they slew the first living creature that they found, in whose blood they not only bathed their swords, but also tasted thereof with their mouths with no less religion and assurance conceived, than if they had already been sure of some notable and fortunate victory. When they saw their own blood run from them in the fight, they waxed never a whit astonished with the matter, but rather doubling their courage with more eagerness they assailed their enemies. (p. 24)

Although Shakespeare's Lady Macbeth retains some of the fierceness of her ancient predecessors, she lacks their taste for blood. The obsessive theme of her sleepwalking, in fact, will be her repeated, futile efforts to wash what she calls the 'damned spots' of Duncan's blood from her hands (5.1). Here, as in her preparation for Duncan's murder, Shakespeare's eleventh-century Scotswoman rehearses a prototypically modern conception of universal femininity, proving once again in her madness that killing is antithetical to woman's essential nature. In the words of the eighteenth-century English actress Sarah Siddons, most celebrated for her portrayal of Lady Macbeth, the lady's 'feminine nature, her delicate structure, it is too evident, are soon overwhelmed by the enormous pressure of her crimes'.[11]

Shakespeare's antithesis between women's milk and murder, which also became an essential feature of Lady Macbeth's character, required an even more radical revision of his source. In the 'Description of Scotland', lactation is not opposed to killing; the two, in fact, are associated. Those same bloodthirsty women of ancient Scotland, according to the chronicler,

would take intolerable pains to bring up and nourish their own children ...
nay they feared lest they should degenerate and grow out of kind, except they gave them suck themselves, and eschewed strange milk, *therefore* in labor and painfulness they were equal, & neither sex regarded the heat in summer or cold in winter, but traveled barefooted.[12]

Here maternal breastfeeding is evidence both of the women's physical hardiness and of the equality of the sexes in a primitive culture that lived close to nature. This passage in the chronicle is not illustrated, but a very similar conception of ancient Scotswomen seems to lie behind 'the true picture of a woman neighbour to the Picts' that was published in Thomas Hariot's *A Brief and True Report of the New Found Land of Virginia* (London, 1590). The woman in the picture is armed, scantily dressed, and barefooted, and the caption explains, 'they let hang their breasts out, as for the rest they did carry such weapons as the men did, and were as good as the men for the war' (see Figure 5).

Neither the chronicle nor the play offers a reliable picture of ancient Scotswomen. Both are inflected by sixteenth- and seventeenth-century debates about breastfeeding—and also by changing conceptions of women's place in the world, and the basis of gender itself. Historians of sexual difference have argued that 'sex as we know it was invented' some time 'in the eighteenth century', but the modern conception of sexual difference that Thomas Laqueur identifies as the 'two-sex model'[13] seems clearly anticipated in Shakespeare's representation of Lady Macbeth. For although both the chronicler and the playwright can be said to advocate maternal breastfeeding, their advocacy takes strikingly different forms. In the chronicle it is a means by which the strong mothers of ancient Scotland produced strong offspring; in *Macbeth* it is a distinctively female activity which expresses the gendered gentleness that is the natural disposition of all women in every time and place.

Because this conception of womanhood has become so well established, Shakespeare's characterization of Lady Macbeth has been both accessible and acceptable to modern audiences. But it would not have seemed so familiar at the beginning of the seventeenth century. In fact, Shakespeare's Lady Macbeth differs as much from the women of the playwright's own time as she does from the ancient Scotswomen described in his chronicle source. In another speech frequently cited in modern criticism, Lady Macbeth states that she has 'given suck, and know[s] | How tender 'tis to love the babe that milks me' (1.7.54–5), but a real woman of Lady Macbeth's station would have been extremely unlikely to do so at the time the play was written. The tradition of using wetnurses was so widely accepted in the sixteenth

5. 'The true picture of a woman neighbour to the Picts', from Thomas Hariot, *A Brief and True Report of the New Found Land of Virginia* (1590)

and seventeenth centuries that 'wealthy [and aristocratic] mothers who decided to nurse their own babies were regarded as extraordinary'.[14] In John Webster's early seventeenth-century play *The White Devil* (1610–12), for instance, maternal breastfeeding provides the final touch in the playwright's portrait of Brachiano's long-suffering wife, Isabella, as an incredibly selfless woman. Murdered by order of her faithless husband, Isabella is fervently mourned by her son Giovanni:

> I have often heard her say she gave me suck
> And it should seem by that she dearly loved me
> Since princes seldom do it.
>
> (3.2.336–9)

Seventeenth-century tombstones also record instances of maternal breastfeeding as exceptional examples of motherly devotion. The memorial brass to Elizabeth Brand and her husband, for instance, recorded in 1638 that the couple had left 'their rare examples to 6 sons and 6 daughters (all nursed with her unborrowed milk)'. The 1658 monument to Lady Essex, Countess of Manchester, records that she 'left 8 children 6 sons & 2 daughters 7 of them she nursed with her own breasts'.[15]

Testimonials such as these were rare, not only because maternal breastfeeding was exceptional but also because it was more often discouraged than celebrated. In 1598, for example, when the sister of one of Queen Elizabeth's ladies in waiting decided to nurse her own child, her father wrote, 'I am sorry that yourself will needs nurse her', and the child's godfather wrote, 'I should like nothing that you play the nurse if you were my wife'. Husbands in particular often objected to maternal breastfeeding, for a number of reasons.[16] Even if the Galenic injunction that nursing women should abstain from sexual relations was ignored, other issues remained: the husband's interest in his wife's company and productive and reproductive labour and concerns about the preservation of the mother's health and beauty. The erotic ideal of small, high, rounded breasts was inconsistent with lactation: the tight corsets that were used to produce beautiful breasts could also produce inverted nipples, which made nursing difficult, and if the lady did manage to nurse, the appearance of her breasts would be 'ruined'.

The controversy persisted for hundreds of years. Prince Henry heard a disputation on the subject at Oxford in 1605,[17] and it was not until the second half of the eighteenth century that maternal breastfeeding became the normal custom in England.[18] Nonetheless, by the time Shakespeare wrote *Macbeth*, there was already a growing chorus of authoritative voices urging Englishwomen to breastfeed their own children.[19] In 1580, for instance, Thomas Tusser had recommended,

> Good housewives take pain, and do count it good luck
> to make their own breast their own child to give suck.
> Though wrauling [i.e. quarrelling] and rocking be noisome so near,
> yet lost by ill nursing is worser to hear.
> But one thing I warn thee, let housewife be nurse
> lest husband do find thee too frank with his purse.[20]

Tusser gives practical arguments for maternal nursing: children sent out to wetnurses are less likely to survive, and a husband is less likely to complain about a wife's extravagance if she provides free milk for the children. Other advocates for maternal nursing decried mercenary motives (and in fact ascribed them to the poor wetnurses and not to the more affluent parents), resting their appeals instead on ethical and religious grounds. Erasmus's colloquy 'The New Mother' (1526), for instance, a curious combination of arguments for maternal nursing and instruction on the nature of the soul, argued that the nurse may have 'neither good health nor good morals and . . . may be much more concerned about a bit of money than about a whole baby'. 'Children's characters', Erasmus explains, 'are injured by the nature of the milk just as in fruits or plants the moisture of the soil changes the quality of what it nourishes. Or do you suppose the common saying, "He drank in his spite with his nurse's milk" has no basis?' (pp. 273, 283).

Puritans were especially opposed to the use of wetnurses. The most popular and influential early seventeenth-century Puritan writers on household management—Robert Cleaver, John Dod, William Gouge, and William Perkins—all strongly advocated maternal breastfeeding.[21] Their advocacy seems to have had some effect, because although the use of wetnurses persisted—and in fact even increased—during the seventeenth century, social historians have noted that women who belonged to the strictest Protestant sects were apparently most likely to breastfeed their own children, even when compared to other women who occupied similar social stations (Fildes, p. 99). Elizabeth Clinton recorded her own response to their preaching when she wrote *The Countess of Lincoln's Nursery* (1622). As the title implies, Clinton was an aristocrat, and her book contains the only recorded condemnation of wetnursing by an aristocratic woman during the period. Writing as a widow with grown children, Clinton explains that she had not breastfed her own children 'partly [because] I was over-ruled by another's authority and partly deceived by some ill counsel, and partly I had not so well considered of my duty in this motherly office as since I did, when it was too late for me to put it in execution'. Now convinced that it was 'the express ordinance of God that mothers should nurse their own children' and that failure to do so was a sin, she published her treatise on breastfeeding both as a tribute to her daughter-in-law, who did nurse her own children, and in the hopes that other young women would see the light.[22]

The growing insistence that women should nurse their own children can thus be seen as part of a Protestant redefinition of family life, but it can also be seen as part of a larger cultural project at the beginning of the modern era to institute gender as the essential axis of difference between people and to confine women within the household, which was being redefined as a private, domestic space, separate from the public world of masculine activity. 'Motherhood', as Susan Cahn points out, 'was increasingly presented by ministers, and accepted by the laity as so vital—and time-consuming—a chore that it was a "special vocation".' A less idealized explanation comes from a citizen wife in Thomas Dekker and John Webster's play *Westward Ho* (1607), who denounces demands for maternal nursing as 'the policy of husbands to keep their Wives in' (1.2.116–17) (Cahn, pp. 104–6).

So long as motherhood and breastfeeding were seen as separate functions, different classes of women were assumed to perform different sorts of productive and reproductive labour. In 1592, Gervase Babington had advised women to decide whether or not to nurse '*according to your place* and other true circumstance'.[23] As Gail Paster observes, 'the institution of wet-nursing enforced a major...difference...between women of different stations'.[24] Because lactation has a contraceptive effect, the use of wetnurses to feed the babies of wealthy and aristocratic women helped to produce significant differences in fertility, enabling wealthy families, in effect, to appropriate the fertility of the poor. In one Somerset parish, for instance, Dorothy McLaren found that the fourteen rich women, 'who almost certainly' used wetnurses, had a fertility rate double that of the parish mothers 'overall'.[25]

For the rich, wetnursing served the need to produce heirs. For the women who served as wetnurses, it acted as a restraint on fertility. For families of the middling sort, wetnursing served an additional function, since it enabled mothers to continue performing work that increased the wealth of the family. As we have seen in Chapter 2, William Gouge, an advocate of maternal breastfeeding, believed that the obligation of maternal nursing should take precedence over economic expediency or a husband's desires because it was a 'special calling' ordained by God, but he nonetheless recognized that, as he wrote, 'a mother that hath a trade or that hath the care of an house will neglect much business by nursing her child: and her husband will save more by giving half a crown a week to a nurse, than if his wife gave the child suck'.

Even this brief survey shows that the campaign for maternal breastfeeding had numerous rationales, often inconsistent with each other. Religious arguments and appeals to nature tended to emphasize gender differences at the expense of social and economic distinctions by insisting that *all* women, regardless of their station, should breastfeed their own children. On the other hand, many sixteenth- and seventeenth-century advocates for maternal nursing based their arguments on the need to maintain the social hierarchy. Erasmus was not the only authority who warned that infants would imbibe 'low' habits and dispositions from their nurses; and wetnursing did in fact produce cross-class bonds which sometimes persisted into adult life, and even beyond, as many people remembered their old wetnurses in their wills (Fildes, pp. 162, 202). In most cases, the infant lived in the nurse's household. In all cases wetnursing entailed an intimate, physical relationship between child and nurse. The nurse, moreover, was likely to be the person to teach the perhaps aristocratic and certainly wealthier infant its 'mother tongue'.

With the advantage of hindsight, however, the growing demand that all mothers breastfeed their own children can be seen as part of the long-term project of denying class difference in an ideology of universal humanity, differentiated only by gender—with the same modernizing project that produced the ideal of the domesticated wife. The traditional use of wetnurses divided the poor families whose women did the wetnursing from their social and economic superiors. The new requirement that all mothers nurse their own children emphasized instead the distinctions between men and women—the division between the male domain of public economic and political action and the female enclosure of private, domestic affairs. This is not to say that all women have ever been enclosed within the household. Even women who might have preferred domesticity have been forced by economic necessity to work outside their homes; but the ideal of woman's 'natural' and 'traditional' place at home is undisturbed by that reality. The only division that 'counts' is the 'natural' division between men and women that was to become one of the salient features of modernity.

Here too, Shakespeare's anachronistic rendering of his eleventh-century story is revealing. Instead of accompanying her husband into battle like the ancient Scotswomen in the chronicle, Lady Macbeth waits at home for his letter and his return like a good, modern wife. In fact, the domestication of women appears to be a major project of this play. The only women who appear outside the enclosed walls of their homes are the weird sisters, and Shakespeare transforms his source material to emphasize that they are both unnatural and unwomanly. He places their initial—and never-contested—description in the mouth of Banquo, whom he depicts as a reliable informant, a prudent and sympathetic character who will shortly show the good judgement and moral fortitude to resist the temptations offered by the witches' prophecies.

Banquo asks,

> What are these,
> So withered, and so wild in their attire,
> That look not like th'inhabitants o'th' earth
> And yet are on't?

$$(1.3.37-40)$$

This description identifies the weird sisters as unnatural, but the evidence of their unwomanliness receives even more emphasis, since it is reserved for the end of the speech: 'You should be women', Banquo concludes, 'And yet your beards forbid me to interpret | That you are so' (1.3.43–5). These beards have received considerable attention in recent criticism because their significance as visible, physical marks of the witches' defective femininity is clearly legible in modern terms. In Holinshed's *Chronicles*, by contrast, their prototypes are unequivocally female. They are described as 'three women in strange and wild apparel, resembling creatures of elder world' met by Macbeth and Banquo as they are 'passing through the woods and fields' (5:268). In the 1577 edition the description is illustrated with a woodcut depicting two bearded men on horseback encountering three attractive and elaborately gowned women. Instead of Shakespeare's 'blasted heath' (1.3.77), the illustration shows a landscape embellished with vegetation, including a large tree in full leaf. One of the women has prominent breasts and visible nipples, but there is no sign of the beards that have received so much attention from recent critics. Banquo's often-quoted reference to their embodied gender ambiguity is entirely Shakespeare's invention (see Figure 6).

Shakespeare's representation of the witches' gender as physically compromised transformed his historical source to express the prototypically modern assumption that the qualities of gentleness and pity are naturally grounded in women's bodies—the same assumption that forms the basis of Lady Macbeth's desire to be 'unsexed' so she can commit the murder of Duncan. The same assumptions about female sexuality can also be seen in the fascination of post-Shakespearian readers with the issue of Lady Macbeth's motherhood. If, as she says, she has 'given suck', then where is the baby, and why does Macbeth complain that the royal sceptre he has acquired is 'barren' (3.1.63)? Questions like these were famously discredited by L. C. Knights in his satiric essay *How Many Children Had Lady Macbeth?* (1933),[26] but they persist because motherhood is now generally regarded as the necessary fulfilment of a woman's 'nature'—an assumption that is already adumbrated in Shakespeare's playscript, where both Lady Macbeth and the weird sisters are associated with infanticide. Urging Macbeth to steel his resolve for Duncan's slaughter, Lady Macbeth declares,

> I have given suck, and know
> How tender 'tis to love the babe that milks me.
> I would, while it was smiling in my face,
> Have plucked my nipple from his boneless gums
> And dashed the brains out, had I so sworn
> As you have done to this.
>
> (1.7.54–9)

The Historie of Scotlande. 243

was right displeasant to him and his people, as shoulde appeare in that it was a custome many yeares after, that no Knightes were made in Norway, excepte they were firste sworne to revenge the slaughter of theyr countreymen and frendes thus slayne in Scotland.

The Scottes having wonne so notable a victory, after they had gathered and divided the spoyle of the fielde, caused solemne processions to be made in all places of the realme, and thankes to be given to almightie God, that had sent them so fayre a day over their enimies.

But whylest the people were thus at theyr processions, worde was brought that a newe fleete of Danes was arrived at Kingcorne, sent thyther by Canute king of England in revenge of his brothers Suenoes overthrow.

To resist these enimies, whiche were already landed, and busie in spoiling the countrey, Makbeth and Banquho were sente with the kings authoritie, who having with them a convenient power, encountred the enimies, slewe parte of them, and chased the other to their shippes. They that escaped and got once to theyr shippes, obtayned of Makbeth for a great summe of golde, that suche of theyr freendes as were slaine at this last bickering might be buried in Saint Colmes Inche. In memorie whereof, many olde Sepultures are yet in the sayde Inche, there to be seene graven with the armes of the Danes, as the maner of burying noble men still is, and heretofore hath bene used.

A peace was also concluded at the same time betwixte the Danes and Scottishmen, ratified as some have wrytten in this wise. That from thence forth the Danes shoulde never come into Scotlande to make any warres agaynst the Scottes by any maner of meanes. *A peace concluded betwixt Scottes and Danes.*

And these were the warres that Duncane had with forrayne enimies in the seventh yeare of his reygne.

Shortly after happened a straunge and uncouth wonder, whiche afterwarde was the cause of muche trouble in the realme of Scotlande as ye shall after heare. It fortuned as Makbeth & Banquho iourneyed towarde Fores, where the king as then lay, they went sporting by the way togither without other companie, save only themselves, passing through the woodes and fieldes, when sodenly in the middes of a launde, there met them .iij. women in straunge & ferly apparell, resembling creatures of an elder worlde, whom when they attentively behelde, wondering much at the sight, The first of them spake & sayde: All hayle Makbeth Thane of Glammis (for he had lately entred into that dignitie and office by the death of his father Synel.) The .ij. of them said: Hayle Makbeth Thane of Cawder: but the third sayde: All hayle Makbeth that hereafter shall be king of Scotland. *The prophesie of three women supposing to be the weird sisters or feiries.*

Then Banquho, what maner of women (saith he) are you, that seeme so litle favourable unto me, where as to my fellow here, besides highe offices, yee assigne also the kingdome, appointyng forth nothing for me at all? Yes sayth the firste of them, wee promise greater benefites unto thee, than unto him, for he shall reygne in in deede, but with an unluckie ende: neyther shall he leave any issue behinde him to succeede in his place, where contrarily thou in deede shalt not reygne at all, but of thee those shall be borne whiche shall governe the Scottishe kingdome by long order of continuall discent. Herewith the foresayde women vanished immediatly out of theyr sight. This was reputed at the first but some vayne fantasticall illusion by Makbeth and Banquho, in so muche that Banquho woulde call Makbeth in ieste kyng of *A thing to wonder at.*

Q.ij. Scot-

6. Macbeth and Banquo meet the weird sisters, as illustrated in Holinshed's *Chronicles of England, Scotland and Ireland* (1577)

Similarly, the gruesome ingredients in the witches' cauldron include the finger of a 'birth-strangled babe | Ditch-delivered by a drab' (4.1. 30–1).

As we have seen in Chapter 2, the restriction of women to the private, domestic sphere, defined by their 'natural' vocation as wives and mothers, which was to become a leading feature of modernity, was only beginning in Shakespeare's time; and many of Shakespeare's plays had an uneasy relation to emergent notions of women's nature. Devoted mothers are notoriously difficult to find. There are far more fathers than mothers, and the mothers who do appear are usually unsatisfactory. Both Mistress Page and Lady Capulet choose undesirable mates for their daughters. Gertrude thwarts Hamlet's hopes for the Danish crown. Volumnia is directly responsible for her son's ruin. Looking for an example of Cleopatra's maternal devotion, Mrs Rosa Grindon, the Victorian apologist for Shakespeare's female characters, could find only 'one strong touch given to us of Cleopatra as a mother. To gratify her he [Antony] gives kingdoms to her sons, as peace-offerings.'[27]

In *Macbeth*, there is one female character who has a living child, and although her role is minor, she constitutes the norm of 'natural' femininity against which both the witches and Lady Macbeth are measured. Here too Shakespeare had to modify his source, which gave no indication of Lady Macduff's character but simply recorded her murder, along with the rest of Macduff's household. According to the *Chronicles*, Macbeth

came hastily with a great power into Fife, and forthwith besieged the castle where Macduff dwelled, trusting to have found him therein. They that kept the house, without any resistance opened the gates, and suffered him to enter, mistrusting none evil. But nevertheless Macbeth most cruelly caused the wife and children of Macduff, with all other whom he found in that castle to be slain. (5:274)

Instead of the mistaken trust of Macduff's household, Shakespeare emphasizes the feminine helplessness of Macduff's wife, a woman whose husband has 'unnaturally' left her unprotected in a dangerous situation. 'He loves us not', she complains, 'he wants the natural touch; for the poor wren, | The most diminutive of birds, will fight, | Her young ones in her nest, against the owl' (4.2.8–11). Instead of

following the wren's example, however, she simply announces her
female weakness:

> Whither should I fly?
> I have done no harm. But.... why...
> Do I put up that womanly defence,
> To say I have done no harm?
>
> (4.2.73–9)

Significantly, the Folio speech headings designate Lady Macduff
throughout the scene simply as 'Wife'. A medieval noblewoman
would have been expected to lead the defence of the castle in
her husband's absence, but this lady is represented as a domesticated
modern 'wife', helpless without her husband's protection, easy
prey to the assassins who violate her domestic space. In Shakespeare's
script, Macduff's medieval castle seems to be reimagined as a
modern household rather than a feudal stronghold. The chronicle
clearly implies that the castle might have been defended, but no one
in the play seems to entertain that possibility. Ross advises the Lady to
be patient (4.2.2). The Messenger warns her to flee (4.2.67–9). Macduff, hearing of the slaughter, mourns his lost family as helpless
domesticated creatures: 'All my pretty ones? | Did you say all?... What,
all my pretty chickens and their dam | At one fell swoop?' (4.3.217–20).

Although the history Shakespeare stages in *Macbeth* was taken
from Holinshed's *Chronicles*, by the time it got to the Jacobean
stage, it had been updated for current consumption. As we have
seen, however, the process of updating did not end with Shakespeare's
playscript. Thus, although the play seems clearly legible in modern
terms, I do not believe it could have been read the same way at the
beginning of the seventeenth century. When we hear Lady Macbeth
worry that her husband may not be able to murder Duncan because
his 'nature' is 'too full o' th' milk of human kindness' (1.5.14–15), we are
likely to assume that she is afraid he lacks manliness. The text offers
some support for this view: Lady Macbeth herself connects manliness
and murder when Macbeth does in fact attempt to back out of their
agreement to murder the king, rebuking him, 'when you durst do it,
then you were a man' (1.7.49). However, the definition of 'manliness'
is a subject of repeated contestation in the playscript. Even here,

Macbeth has just argued, 'I dare do all that may become a man; | Who dares do more is none' (1.7.46–7).

This is not the only place where Shakespeare's script offers significant resistances to the kind of seamless, ideologically familiar construction I have been suggesting because the ideological regime it prefigures—and indeed helped to produce—was only beginning to take shape. Consider, for instance, the modern ideal of a loving, companionate marriage, an innovation by no means universally celebrated in Shakespeare's time, and certainly not in his plays. Although marriage constitutes the desired resolution in most of his comedies, he offers very few models of marital bliss; and the married couples he does depict are often troubling to modern assumptions that happy and successful marriages are the results of personal virtue and good mental health, since they are rarely associated with admirable characters. Perhaps the best marriage of all in modern terms is the adulterous union between Gertrude and the villainous usurper who murdered her former husband, because even in middle age they seem to enjoy the shared sexual passion which is now regarded as a healthy achievement and the hallmark of a successful marriage. In *Macbeth*, the villain-hero and his wife have a remarkable mutuality of purpose and emotional intimacy when they conspire to murder Duncan. The virtuous Macduffs never even appeared together on stage until Davenant rewrote the play for Restoration audiences. Davenant had to add three new scenes, where Lady Macduff was shown as her husband's confidant, advisor, and inspiration, in order to ensure that the good people would have a good, modern marriage.

Davenant made numerous revisions, designed, like these, to update the story for a new audience. His modernized version held the stage for over a century.[28] Significantly, one place where he did *not* feel the need to revise was the soliloquy in which Lady Macbeth called on the spirits to 'unsex' her, which Davenant imported substantially unchanged into the new script. Its meaning must have seemed clear and contemporary (or perhaps I should say 'dateless') because now it could be performed by a female actor, Mrs Betterton, who really did have a woman's breasts.

Davenant's production marks a milestone in the history of ideological reconstruction that has recruited Shakespeare's female characters in the service of a recognizably modern gender ideology and the constricting stereotypes it requires. Simply exposing that history for what it is can help to break the hold of its products over our own imaginations, but much more remains to be done. The reason the succession of shapes that Shakespeare's women have assumed offers a revealing window into our own history is that each of those shapes served as a mirror for whatever images of women's nature and experience were conceivable at the time of their production. If changing the ways we imagine Shakespeare's women will help us to change the ways we imagine ourselves, the reverse is also true. The women we see in his plays are inevitably limited by the range of possibilities we can imagine for ourselves.

Further Reading

Chapter 1

The foundation of twentieth-century feminist Shakespeare criticism—and a book that still repays careful reading—is Juliet Dusinberre's *Shakespeare and the Nature of Women*, originally published in 1975 (third edition, New York: Palgrave Macmillan, 2003). The optimistic views of Dusinberre and other contemporary feminists concerning women's place in the drama and society of Shakespeare and his contemporaries were vigorously challenged by Lisa Jardine in *Still Harping on Daughters: Women and Drama in the Age of Shakespeare* (Brighton: Harvester, 1983). For a useful overview of the early progress of twentieth-century feminist Shakespeare criticism, see the Introduction and Selective Bibliography in *The Woman's Part: Feminist Criticism of Shakespeare*, edited by Carolyn Ruth Swift Lenz, Gayle Greene, and Carol Thomas Neely (Urbana: University of Illinois Press, 1980); and Philip C. Kolin's *Shakespeare and Feminist Criticism: An Annotated Bibliography and Commentary* (New York and London: Garland, 1991), which covers the years from 1977 to 1988. The current state of feminist Shakespeare criticism is well represented in Dympna Callaghan's richly varied anthology, *A Feminist Companion to Shakespeare* (Oxford: Blackwell, 2000). For a historical survey of earlier women's responses to Shakespeare, see *Women Reading Shakespeare 1660–1900: An Anthology of Criticism*, edited by Ann Thompson and Sasha Roberts (Manchester: Manchester University Press, 1997).

One of the earliest and most influential readings of Elizabethan culture and of Shakespeare's plays that stresses the anxieties of men confronted by female authority and power is Louis Adrian Montrose's article *'A Midsummer Night's Dream* and the Shaping Fantasies of Elizabethan Culture: Gender, Power, Form', in Margaret W. Ferguson, Maureen Quilligan, and Nancy J. Vickers (eds.), *Rewriting the Renaissance: The Discourses of Sexual Difference in Early Modern Europe* (Chicago: University of Chicago Press, 1986), pp. 179–86. Later studies include Mark Breitenberg's book, *Anxious Masculinity in Early Modern England* (Cambridge: Cambridge University Press, 1996) and Steven Mullaney's article, 'Mourning and Misogyny: *Hamlet, The Revenger's Tragedy,* and the Final Progress of Elizabeth I, 1600–1607', *Shakespeare Quarterly,* 45 (1994), pp. 139–62.

Impressive documentation of women's agency during the late sixteenth and early seventeenth centuries can be found in Margaret Ezell, *The Patriarch's*

Wife: Literary Evidence and the History of the Family (Chapel Hill: University
of North Carolina Press, 1987), which demonstrates the prominent roles
played by women in arranging marriages; Laura Gowing, *Domestic Dangers:
Women, Words, and Sex in Early Modern London* (Oxford: Clarendon Press,
1996), which examines the records of women's litigation in London; and Amy
Louise Erickson, *Women and Property in Early Modern England* (London:
Routledge, 1993), which documents the widespread economic power and
activity of early modern Englishwomen.

Chapter 2

The definitive account of the role of clothing in Renaissance culture is Ann
Rosalind Jones and Peter Stallybrass, *Renaissance Clothing and the Materials of
Memory* (Cambridge: Cambridge University Press, 2000). On women's cloth-
ing during the Middle Ages and Renaissance, other useful resources are 'The
Body, Appearance, and Sexuality', by Sara F. Matthews Grieco, in Natalie
Zemon Davis and Arlette Farge (eds.), *A History of Women in the West*, Vol.
III (Cambridge, Mass.: Belknap Press of Harvard University Press, 1993); and
François Boucher, *20,000 Years of Fashion: The History of Costume and Personal
Adornment* (New York: Harry N. Abrams, 1987). For a detailed survey of the
English laws that regulated apparel during Shakespeare's time, see Wilfred
Hooper, 'The Tudor Sumptuary Laws', *English Historical Review*, 30 (1915),
pp. 433–49.

There has been a wealth of excellent feminist scholarship on Queen Eliza-
beth I in recent years. Carole Levin's *The Heart and Stomach of a King:
Elizabeth I and the Politics of Sex and Power* (Philadelphia: University of
Pennsylvania Press, 1994) offers a richly documented and nuanced account of
responses to the Queen by her contemporaries. Susan Frye provides an incisive
analysis of the implications of the competing images of Queen Elizabeth in
Elizabeth I: The Competition for Representation (New York and Oxford: Oxford
University Press, 1993), pp. 3–21. For an analysis of the ways Elizabeth used her
gender in the construction of her royal authority, see chapter 2, 'Gender and
the Construction of Royal Authority in the Speeches of Elizabeth I' in Mary
Beth Rose's *Gender and Heroism in Early Modern English Literature* (Chicago:
University of Chicago Press, 2002). For a thoughtful defence of the recent
scholarly emphasis on negative responses to Elizabeth, see 'The Dark Side of
the Cult of Elizabeth', Julia M. Walker's introduction to her anthology *Dissing
Elizabeth: Negative Representations of Gloriana* (Durham and London: Duke
University Press, 1998). The standard older biography is J. E. Neale's *Queen
Elizabeth I* (Chicago: Academy Chicago Publishers, 1999), originally pub-
lished in 1934 under the title of *Queen Elizabeth*.

There are numerous studies of Shakespeare's life, but a good starting place is S. Schoenbaum's *William Shakespeare: A Documentary Life* (New York: Oxford University Press, 1977). This is an abridged version of the book cited in note 9 on page 149. A detailed, readable account of the environment in which Shakespeare lived his early years can be found in Jeanne Jones, *Family Life in Shakespeare's England 1570–1630* (Stratford-upon-Avon: The Shakespeare Birthplace Trust, 1996). Mark Eccles's *Shakespeare in Warwickshire* (Madison: University of Wisconsin Press, 1961) focuses on the records that reveal the traces of Shakespeare's life in Stratford, especially those of his family, neighbours, schoolmasters, and friends. Recent biographical studies include Park Honan's *Shakespeare: A Life* (Oxford: Oxford University Press, 1998), which offers a readable narrative, and Stanley Wells's magisterial *Shakespeare For All Time* (London: Macmillan, 2002), which includes extensive information about Shakespeare's life as a working playwright in London and about the afterlife of both the plays and the playwright. Equally authoritative but more concise are the first two chapters in Wells's *Shakespeare: A Life in Drama* (New York: Norton, 1995). Katherine Duncan-Jones's *Ungentle Shakespeare: Scenes From His Life* (London: Arden, 2001) offers a provocative argument for Shakespeare's human fallibility in regard to such matters as his financial dealings, his ambition, and his sexual relationships.

A well-documented survey of women's lives in Tudor and Stuart England that ranges widely across the social spectrum is Sara Mendelson and Patricia Crawford's *Women in Early Modern England 1550–1720* (Oxford: Clarendon Press, 1998). For reliable short introductions to current thinking about the early modern English household, see Susan Dwyer Amussen, 'The Family and the Household', in David Scott Kastan (ed.), *A Companion to Shakespeare* (Oxford: Blackwell, 1999); Diana E. Henderson, 'The Theatre and Domestic Culture', in John D. Cox and David Scott Kastan (eds.), *A New History of Early English Drama* (New York: Columbia University Press, 1997); and Mario DiGangi, 'The Social Relations of Shakespeare's Comic Households', in Richard Dutton and Jean E. Howard (eds.), *A Companion to Shakespeare's Works, Volume III: The Comedies* (Oxford: Blackwell, 2003). For richly detailed, scholarly studies of the reduction of the household in late sixteenth- and early seventeenth-century thought to a feminized private space that anticipates modern domestic mythologies, see Lena Cowen Orlin, *Private Matters and Public Culture in Post-Reformation England* (Ithaca: Cornell University Press, 1994) and Natasha Korda, *Shakespeare's Domestic Economies: Gender and Property in Early Modern England* (Philadelphia: University of Pennsylvania Press, 2002). For studies of the redefinition and restriction of women's work during the sixteenth and seventeenth centuries, see Alice Clark, *Working Life of Women in the Seventeenth Century* (third edition,

London and New York: Routledge, 1992) and Susan Cahn, *Industry of Devotion: The Transformation of Women's Work in England, 1500–1660* (New York: Columbia University Press, 1987). Other useful studies of women's work and women's roles in the public sphere in late medieval and early modern England include Judith M. Bennett, *Ale, Beer and Brewsters in England: Women's Work in a Changing World, 1300–1600* (New York: Oxford University Press, 1996); Diane Willen, 'Women in the Public Sphere in Early Modern England: The Case of the Urban Working Poor', *Sixteenth Century Journal*, XIX, 4 (1988), pp. 559–75, and Merry E. Wiesner, 'Women's Defense of Their Public Role', in *Women in the Middle Ages and the Renaissance*, edited by Mary Beth Rose (Syracuse: Syracuse University Press, 1986), pp. 1–27.

On women's involvement in English Renaissance theatrical production, see Ann Thompson, 'Women/"women" and the stage' in *Women and Literature in Britain 1500–1700* (Cambridge: Cambridge University Press, 1996), edited by Helen Wilcox; Susan Cerasano and Marion Wynne-Davies, *Renaissance Drama by Women: Texts and Documents* (London and New York: Routledge, 1996), and *Readings in Renaissance Women's Drama: Criticism, History, and Performance 1594–1998* (London and New York: Routledge, 1998); Natasha Korda, 'Household Property/Stage Property: Henslowe as Pawnbroker', *Theatre Journal*, 48: 2 (May 1996); James Stokes, 'Women and Mimesis in Medieval and Renaissance Somerset (and Beyond)', *Comparative Drama*, 7 (summer 1993), pp. 176–96; and *Women Players in England, 1500–1660: Beyond the All-Male Stage*, edited by Pamela Allen Brown and Peter Parolin (Burlington, Vt.: Ashgate, 2005).

On women's presence in Shakespeare's original audiences, see Jean E. Howard, *The Stage and Social Struggle in Early Modern England* (London: Routledge, 1994); Alfred Harbage, *Shakespeare's Audience* (New York: Columbia University Press, 1941); Andrew Gurr, *Playgoing in Shakespeare's London* (third edition, Cambridge: Cambridge University Press, 2004); and Richard Levin, 'Women in the Renaissance Theatre Audience', *Shakespeare Quarterly*, 40 (1989), pp. 165–74.

Chapter 3

On modern productions of *The Taming of the Shrew*, see Penny Gay, *As She Likes It*, chapter 3: '*The Taming of the Shrew*: Avoiding the Feminist Challenge'; and Diana E. Henderson, 'A Shrew for the Times', in *Shakespeare, the Movie: Popularizing the Plays on Film, TV, and Video*, edited by Lynda E. Boose and Richard Burt (London: Routledge, 1997). On the stage history of the play, see Tori Haring-Smith, *From Farce to Metadrama: A Stage History of The Taming of the Shrew, 1594–1983* (Westport, Conn.: Greenwood Press,

1985); Elizabeth Schafer's edition of the play in the 'Shakespeare in Production' series (Cambridge: Cambridge University Press, 2002); and Dana E. Aspinall's anthology *The Taming of the Shrew: Critical Essays* (Routledge: New York and London, 2002). An extensive collection of documents illustrating the play's historical context can be found in Frances E. Dolan's excellent edition, *The Taming of the Shrew: Texts and Contexts* (Boston and New York: Bedford Books of St. Martin's Press, 1996). Karen Newman offered an astute feminist analysis of the play, which stresses the impact of the boy actor, in *Fashioning Femininity and English Renaissance Drama* (Chicago: University of Chicago Press, 1991), pp. 33–50.

On the implications of *The Merry Wives of Windsor* for women's history, see Richard Helgerson, 'The Buck Basket, the Witch, and the Queen of Fairies: The Women's World of Shakespeare's Windsor', in *Adulterous Alliances: Home, State, and History in Early Modern European Drama and Painting* (Chicago: University of Chicago Press, 2000); Wendy Wall, 'Why Does Puck Sweep? Shakespearean Fairies and the Politics of Cleaning', in her *Staging Domesticity: Household Work and English Identity in Early Modern Drama* (Cambridge: Cambridge University Press, 2002); Natasha Korda, 'Judicious Oeillades: Supervising Marital Property in *The Merry Wives of Windsor*', in her *Shakespeare's Domestic Economies: Gender and Property in Early Modern England* (Philadelphia: University of Pennsylvania Press, 2002), pp. 76–110; and Lena Cowen Orlin, 'Shakespearean Comedy and Material Life', in *A Companion to Shakespeare's Works, Volume III: The Comedies*, edited by Richard Dutton and Jean E. Howard (Oxford: Blackwell, 2003).

Chapter 4

Although there have been numerous discussions of the cultural implications of the use of male actors to play women's roles in Shakespeare's theatre, the best is probably Stephen Orgel's *Impersonations: The Performance of Gender in Shakespeare's England* (Cambridge: Cambridge University Press, 1996). For an extensive survey of the use of cross-dressing on the English Renaissance stage, see Michael Shapiro, *Gender in Play on the Shakespearean Stage: Boy Heroines and Female Pages* (Ann Arbor: University of Michigan Press, 1994).

For a well-documented and incisive analysis of the connections between antitheatrical polemic and misogyny, see Jean E. Howard, *The Stage and Social Struggle in Early Modern England* (London: Routledge, 1994). Other useful treatments include Katharine Eisaman Maus, ' "Playhouse Flesh and Blood": Sexual Ideology and the Restoration Actress', *ELH*, 46 (1979), pp. 595–617;

and Laura Levine, *Men in Women's Clothing: Anti-Theatricality and Effemi-nization 1579–1642* (Cambridge: Cambridge University Press, 1994).

Studies of Shakespeare's Cleopatra that emphasize her reference to the boy actor who played her part include Phyllis Rackin, 'Shakespeare's Boy Cleo-patra, the Decorum of Nature, and the Golden World of Poetry', *PMLA*, 87 (March, 1972), pp. 201–12; Jyotsna Singh, 'Renaissance Anti-Theatricality, Anti-Feminism, and Shakespeare's *Antony and Cleopatra*', *Renaissance Drama*, 20 (1989), pp. 99–119; Madelon Sprengnether, 'The Boy Actor and Femininity in *Antony and Cleopatra*', in *Shakespeare's Personality*, edited by Norman N. Holland *et al.* (Berkeley: University of California Press, 1989), pp. 191–205; and Juliet Dusinberre, 'Squeaking Cleopatras: Gender and Per-formance in *Antony and Cleopatra*', in James C. Bulman (ed.), *Shakespeare: Theory and Performance* (New York: Routledge, 1996), pp. 46–67.

Chapter 5

For a brilliant and influential analysis of the inherent misogyny of the Petrarchan sonnet tradition, see Nancy J. Vickers, 'Diana Described: Scat-tered Woman and Scattered Rhyme', in *Writing and Sexual Difference*, edited by Elizabeth Abel (Chicago: University of Chicago Press, 1982). On the misogyny of Shakespeare's sonnets, see Valerie Traub 'Sex Without Issue: Sodomy, Reproduction, and Signification in Shakespeare's Sonnets', in *Shakespeare's Sonnets: Critical Essays*, edited by James Schiffer (New York: Garland, 2000), pp. 431–52. On the sexual politics of the post-Shakespearian reception of Shakespeare's sonnets, see Peter Stallybrass, 'Editing as Cultural Formation: The Sexing of Shakespeare's Sonnets', *Modern Language Quar-terly*, 54 (1993), and Margreta de Grazia, 'The Scandal of Shakespeare's Sonnets', *Shakespeare Survey*, 46 (1994).

Chapter 6

On post-Shakespearian revisions of the roles of Shakespeare's female char-acters, see Irene G. Dash, *Wooing, Wedding and Power: Women in Shakespeare's Plays* (New York: Columbia University Press, 1981) and *Women's Worlds in Shakespeare's Plays* (Cranbury, NJ: Associated University Presses, 1997). On the impact of twentieth-century gender politics on the staging of Shake-speare's comic heroines, see Penny Gay, *As She Likes It: Shakespeare's Unruly Women* (London: Routledge, 1994). For an excellent feminist psychoanalytic study of *Macbeth*, see Janet Adelman, *Suffocating Mothers: Fantasies of Maternal Origin in Shakespeare's Plays, Hamlet to The Tempest* (New York:

Routledge, 1992), pp. 130–47. For a thoughtful meditation on the significance of references to women's breasts on Shakespeare's stage, see Peter Stallybrass, 'Transvestism and the "body beneath": Speculating on the boy actor', in Susan Zimmerman (ed.), *Erotic Politics: Desire on the Renaissance Stage* (London: Routledge, 1992), pp. 64–83.

Notes

INTRODUCTION

1. Hayden White, *Tropics of Discourse: Essays in Cultural Criticism* (Baltimore and London: The Johns Hopkins University Press, 1978).
2. This and all subsequent quotations from Shakespeare's text come from *The Norton Shakespeare: Based on the Oxford Edition*, edited by Stephen Greenblatt *et al.* (New York: W. W. Norton, 1997).

CHAPTER 1

1. Lena Cowen Orlin, 'A Case for Anecdotalism in Women's History: The Witness Who Spoke when the Cock Crowed', *English Literary Renaissance*, 32 (Winter 2001), p. 75.
2. Steven Mullaney, 'Mourning and Misogyny: *Hamlet, The Revenger's Tragedy*, and the Final Progress of Elizabeth I, 1600–1607', *Shakespeare Quarterly*, 45 (1994), p. 141.
3. N. H. Keeble, *The Cultural Identity of Seventeenth-Century Woman: A Reader* (London: Routledge, 1994), p. 186.
4. Anthony Fletcher, *Gender, Sex and Subordination in England 1500–1800* (New Haven and London: Yale University Press, 1995), pp. 120–2.
5. Karen Newman, *Fashioning Femininity and English Renaissance Drama* (Chicago: University of Chicago Press, 1991), p. 40.
6. Frances E. Dolan, 'Reading, Writing, and Other Crimes', in *Feminist Readings of Early Modern Culture: Emerging Subjects*, edited by Valerie Traub, M. Lindsay Kaplan, and Dympna Callaghan (Cambridge: Cambridge University Press, 1996), p. 159.
7. Lynda E. Boose, 'Scolding Brides and Bridling Scolds: Taming the Woman's Unruly Member', *Shakespeare Quarterly*, 42 (1991), p. 195.
8. Peter Stallybrass, 'Patriarchal Territories: The Body Enclosed', in *Rewriting the Renaissance: The Discourses of Sexual Difference in Early Modern Europe*, edited by Margaret W. Ferguson, Maureen Quilligan, and Nancy J. Vickers (Chicago: University of Chicago Press, 1986), pp. 126–7.
9. Valerie Traub, 'Jewels, Statues, and Corpses: Containment of Female Erotic Power', in *Shakespeare and Gender: A History*, edited by Deborah E. Barker and Ivo Kamps (London and New York: Verso, 1995), p. 121.

10. William C. Carroll, 'The Virgin Not: Language and Sexuality in Shakespeare', in Barker and Kamps, p. 184.

11. Sarah Eaton, 'A Woman of Letters: Lavinia in *Titus Andronicus*', in *Shakespearean Tragedy and Gender*, edited by Shirley Nelson Garner and Madelon Sprengnether (Bloomington, Indiana: Indiana University Press, 1996), summarized by Sprengnether, pp. 12–13.

12. The play has been equally popular with the public at large. As Diana Henderson points out in 'A Shrew for the Times' in *Shakespeare the Movie*, edited by Lynda E. Boose and Richard Burt (Routledge: London and New York, 1997), p. 148, there have been more than eighteen screen versions, a number comparable to that for the 'big four' tragedies. In those same years, the Shakespearian comedy that presents the most realistic and sympathetic view of women, *Merry Wives*, has only 69 citations in the *MLA Bibliography*, despite the current interest in social history.

13. C. Leventen, 'Patrimony and Patriarchy in *The Merchant of Venice*', in *The Matter of Difference: Materialist Feminist Criticism of Shakespeare*, edited by Valerie Wayne (Ithaca: Cornell University Press, 1991), p. 75.

14. Stephen Greenblatt, 'Fiction and Friction', in *Shakespearean Negotiations: The Circulation of Social Energy in Renaissance England* (Berkeley: University of California Press, 1988), p. 93.

15. Lisa Jardine, 'Boy Actors, Female Roles, and Elizabethan Eroticism', in *Staging the Renaissance: Reinterpretations of Elizabethan and Jacobean Drama*, edited by David Scott Kastan and Peter Stallybrass (New York and London: Routledge, 1991), p. 61.

16. Leonard Tennenhouse, *Power on Display: The Politics of Shakespeare's Genres* (New York and London: Methuen, 1986), p. 144.

17. Jean E. Howard and Phyllis Rackin, *Engendering a Nation: A Feminist Account of Shakespeare's English Histories* (London and New York: Routledge, 1997), p. 74.

18. G. Blakemore Evans *et al.* (eds.), *The Riverside Shakespeare*, second edition (Boston and New York: Houghton Mifflin, 1997), p. 535.

19. Marvin Spevack, *A Complete and Systematic Concordance to the Works of Shakespeare* (Hildesheim: Georg Olms, 1968).

20. Peter Erickson, *Rewriting Shakespeare, Rewriting Ourselves* (Berkeley: University of California Press, 1991), pp. 73–4.

21. Louis Adrian Montrose, 'The Place of a Brother in *As You Like It*: Social Process and Comic Form', *Shakespeare Quarterly*, 32 (1981), p. 29.

22. Gayle Rubin's 'The Traffic in Women: Notes on the "Political Economy of Sex" ' in *Towards an Anthropology of Women*, edited by Reina Reiter (New York: Monthly Review Press, 1975), pp. 157–210, is a core text for

contemporary feminist/historicist criticism, but, as Stephen Orgel observes, this 'brilliant, classic essay' illustrates how 'even the most powerful feminist analyses are often in collusion with precisely the patriarchal assumptions they undertake to displace'. 'To define Renaissance culture simply as a patriarchy', he explains, is 'to limit one's view to the view the dominant culture took of itself; to assert that within it women were domestic creatures and a medium of exchange is to take Renaissance ideology at its word, and thereby to elide and suppress the large number of women who operated outside the family system, and the explicit social and legal structures that enabled them, in this patriarchy, to do so.' See Stephen Orgel, *Impersonations: The Performance of Gender in Shakespeare's England* (Cambridge: Cambridge University Press, 1996), p. 125.

23. Kathleen McLuskie, 'The Patriarchal Bard: Feminist Criticism and Shakespeare: *King Lear* and *Measure for Measure*', in *Political Shakespeare: Essays in Cultural Materialism*, edited by Jonathan Dollimore and Alan Sinfield, second edition (Ithaca: Cornell University Press, 1994), p. 97.

24. Beatrice Gottlieb, *The Family in the Western World from the Black Death to the Industrial Age* (New York and Oxford: Oxford University Press, 1993), p. 260, quoted by Merry E. Wiesner, in her review essay, 'Danger, Divorce, and Other Family Values', *The Journal of Women's History*, 8: 2 (1996), p. 160.

25. Deborah C. Payne, 'Reified Object or Emergent Professional? Retheorizing the Restoration Actress', in J. Douglas Canfield and Deborah C. Payne (eds.) *Cultural Readings of Restoration and Eighteenth-Century English Theater* (Athens, Georgia, and London: University of Georgia Press, 1995), p. 22.

26. Pierre Bourdieu and Loïc J. D. Wacquant, *An Invitation to Reflexive Sociology* (Chicago: University of Chicago Press, 1992), pp. 69–70.

27. Carol Thomas Neely, ' "Documents in Madness": Reading Madness and Gender in Shakespeare's Tragedies and Early Modern Culture', in Garner and Sprengnether, p. 96.

28. Jean E. Howard, 'The New Historicism in Renaissance Studies', *English Literary Renaissance*, 16 (1986), p. 22.

29. Coppélia Kahn, *Man's Estate: Masculine Identity in Shakespeare* (Berkeley: University of California Press, 1981), pp. 15–17.

30. Catherine Belsey, *The Subject of Tragedy: Identity and Difference in Renaissance Drama* (London: Methuen, 1985), pp. 190–1.

31. Frances E. Dolan, *Dangerous Familiars: Representations of Domestic Crime in England 1550–1700* (Ithaca and London: Cornell University Press, 1994), p. 5.

32. Moreover, men's status as well as women's changed with marriage. Sir Thomas Smith observed in his *De Republica Anglorum* (1583) that 'commonly we do not call any a yeoman, till he be married, and have children, and as it were have some authority among his neighbours' (edited by Mary Dewar (Cambridge: Cambridge University Press, 1982), p. 76); but this statement is much less familiar to modern scholars.

33. Amy Louise Erickson, *Women and Property in Early Modern England* (London and New York: Routledge, 1993), pp. 8–9.

34. Diana E. Henderson, 'The Theater and Domestic Culture', in *A New History of Early English Drama*, edited by John D. Cox and David Scott Kastan (New York: Columbia University Press, 1997), p. 192.

35. Vivien Brodsky Elliott, 'Single Women in the London Marriage Market: Age, Status and Mobility, 1598–1619', in *Marriage and Society: Studies in the Social History of Marriage*, edited by R. B. Outhwaite (New York: St. Martin's Press, 1982), pp. 89, 97. On women's roles in arranging marriages, see Margaret Ezell, *The Patriarch's Wife: Literary Evidence and the History of the Family* (Chapel Hill and London: University of North Carolina Press, 1987).

36. Antonia Fraser, *The Weaker Vessel: Women in Seventeenth-Century England* (New York: Alfred A. Knopf, 1984), p. 231.

37. Pearl Hogrefe, *Women of Action in Tudor England* (Ames, Iowa: Iowa State University Press, 1977).

38. *Hugh Alley's Caveat: The Markets of London in 1598*, edited by Ian Archer, Caroline Barron, and Vanessa Harding (London: London Topographical Society Publication No. 137, 1988).

39. K. D. M. Snell, 'The Apprenticeship of Women', in *Annals of the Labouring Poor: Social Change and Agrarian England, 1660–1900* (Cambridge: Cambridge University Press, 1985), p. 177.

40. Orgel, p. 73; see also K. D. M. Snell, 'The Apprenticeship of Women' (as above) and Alice Clark, *Working Life of Women in the Seventeenth Century*, third edition (London and New York: Routledge, 1992).

41. Phyllis Rackin, 'Anti-Historians: Women's Roles in Shakespeare's Histories', *Theatre Journal*, 37 (1985), p. 341.

42. William Rowley, Thomas Dekker, and John Ford, *The Witch of Edmonton*, edited by Peter Corbin and Douglas Sedge (Manchester: Manchester University Press, 1999).

43. Jean E. Howard, 'Crossdressing, the Theatre, and Gender Struggle in Early Modern England', *Shakespeare Quarterly*, 39 (1988), pp. 439–40. See also Andrew Gurr, *Playgoing in Shakespeare's London*, second edition (Cambridge: Cambridge University Press, 1996), pp. 61–5 and Appendi-

ces 1 and 2; and Richard Levin, 'Women in the Renaissance Theatre Audience', *Shakespeare Quarterly*, 40 (1989), pp. 165–74.

44. E. K. Chambers, *The Elizabethan Stage*, reprint with corrections (Oxford: Clarendon Press, 1951), Vol. I, p. 325.

CHAPTER 2

1. Raymond Williams, *Marxism and Literature* (New York: Oxford University Press, 1977), pp. 121–7.

2. John Stow, *The Chronicles of England, from Brute unto this present year of Christ, 1580* (London: Ralphe Newberie, [1580]), p. 490.

3. J. E. Neale, *Queen Elizabeth I* (Chicago: Academy Chicago Publishers, 1999), p. 64. Neale's book was originally published in 1934 under the title of *Queen Elizabeth*.

4. Neale, pp. 208–9; Roy Strong, *The Cult of Elizabeth* (Berkeley and Los Angeles: University of California Press, 1977), pp. 117–28.

5. 'THE WHOLE ORDER how our Sovereign Lady Queen Elizabeth, was received into the City of Bristol, and the speeches spoken before her presence, at her entry, with the residue of verses and matter that might not be spoken (for distance of the place) but sent in a book over the Water', *The Firste parte of Churchyardes Chippes* (London: Thomas Marshe, 1575).

6. Christopher Morris, *The Tudors* (Glasgow: William Collins, 1986), pp. 167–8.

7. Philippa Berry, *Of Chastity and Power: Elizabethan Literature and the Unmarried Queen* (London: Routledge, 1989), p. 79.

8. Richard S. Dunn, *The Age of Religious Wars, 1559–1689* (New York: W. W. Norton, 1970), p. 37.

9. S. Schoenbaum, *William Shakespeare: A Documentary Life* (New York: Oxford University Press and Scolar Press, 1975), and Park Honan, *Shakespeare: A Life* (Oxford and New York: Oxford University Press, 1998).

10. Carol Thomas Neely, 'Shakespeare's Women: Historical Facts and Dramatic Representations', in *Shakespeare's Personality*, edited by Norman N. Holland *et al.* (Berkeley and Los Angeles: University of California Press, 1989), pp. 117–18.

11. N. W. Alcock and Robert Bearman, 'Discovering Mary Arden's House: Property and Society in Wilmcote, Warwickshire', *Shakespeare Quarterly*, 53 (Spring 2002), p. 58; C. L. Barber and Richard P. Wheeler, 'Shakespeare in the Rising Middle Classes', in Holland *et al.*, p. 19.

12. Amy Louise Erickson, *Women and Property in Early Modern England* (London and New York: Routledge, 1993), pp. 156–7.

13. Sue Wright, ' "Churmaids, Huswyfes and Hucksters": The Employment of Women in Tudor and Stuart Salisbury', *Women and Work in Pre-Industrial England*, edited by Lindsey Charles and Lorna Duffin (Beckenham, Kent: Croom Helm Ltd., 1985), p. 103.

14. *The Private Life of an Elizabethan Lady: The Diary of Lady Margaret Hoby, 1599–1605*, edited by Joanna Moody (Phoenix Mill, Gloucestershire: Sutton Publishing, 1998).

15. Susan Dwyer Amussen, *An Ordered Society: Gender and Class in Early Modern England* (Oxford: Basil Blackwell, 1988), p. 71.

16. Natasha Korda, 'Household Property/Stage Property: Henslowe as Pawnbroker', *Theatre Journal*, 48: 2 (May 1996), p. 190.

17. S. P. Cerasano and Marion Wynne-Davies (eds.), *Renaissance Drama by Women: Texts and Documents* (London and New York: Routledge, 1996), pp. 159, 174–5.

18. Peter Stallybrass, 'Worn Worlds: Clothes and Identity on the Renaissance Stage', in *Subject and Object in Renaissance Culture*, edited by Margreta de Grazia, Maureen Quilligan, and Peter Stallybrass (Cambridge: Cambridge University Press, 1996), p. 295.

19. Alwin Thaler, ' "Minor Actors and Employees in the Elizabethan Theater', *Modern Philology*, 20: 1 (August 1922), p. 54.

20. Gerald Eades Bentley, *The Profession of Player in Shakespeare's Time, 1590–1642* (Princeton: Princeton University Press, 1984), pp. 94–5.

21. For a good introduction to the work of these and other Renaissance women dramatists, see Cerasano and Wynne-Davies and Susan Cerasano and Marion Wynne-Davis *Readings in Renaissance Women's Drama: Criticism, History, and Performance 1594–1998* (London and New York: Routledge, 1998).

22. Virginia Woolf, *A Room of One's Own* (1929; reprinted, New York and London: Harcourt Brace Jovanovich, 1957), p. 51.

23. Jennifer Summit, *Lost Property: The Woman Writer and English Literary History, 1380–1589* (Chicago: University of Chicago Press, 2000), pp. 61–2.

24. Queen Anne can also be said to have invented the Stuart court masque. Modern scholarship on these masques has traditionally focused either on their male designers, Ben Jonson and Inigo Jones, or on their relations to the interests of King James, but as Leeds Barroll has argued, they were actually designed to further the social and political interests of the Queen who sponsored and performed in them, and to showcase the ladies who formed her court. See Barroll's 'Inventing the Stuart Masque', in *The*

Politics of the Stuart Court Masque, edited by David Bevington and Peter Holbrook (Cambridge: Cambridge University Press, 1998), pp. 121–43.

25. In fact, as Gurr points out, he could identify only eighteen instances of named women attending the theatres because in one case the documentary record identifies only a niece of Elizabeth Wybarn, who could have been either Mary Windsor or Margaret Franke. See *Playgoing in Shakespeare's London*, p. 60 and appendix I, pp. 197–212.

CHAPTER 3

1. My quotations from *Edward III* come from G. Blakemore Evans and J. J. M. Tobin (eds.), *The Riverside Shakespeare*, second edition (Boston: Houghton Mifflin, 1997).

2. Jean E. Howard and Phyllis Rackin, *Engendering a Nation: A Feminist Account of Shakespeare's English Histories* (London: Routledge, 1997), pp. 21–6, 217–18.

3. *Theatre at Stratford-upon-Avon, First Supplement to A Catalogue-Index to Productions of the Royal Shakespeare Company, 1979–1993*, edited by Michael Mullin (London: Greenwood Press, 1994), pp. 140–2, 214–17.

4. C. M. Ingleby, L. Toulmin Smith, F. J. Furnivall, and John Munro, *The Shakspere Allusion-Book: A Collection of Allusions to Shakspere from 1591 to 1700* (London: Oxford University Press, 1932), Vol. II, p. 540.

5. Ann Thompson (ed.), *The Taming of the Shrew* (Cambridge: Cambridge University Press, 1984), pp. 17–18.

6. Leah Marcus, 'The Shakespearean Editor as Shrew-Tamer', *English Literary Renaissance*, 22:2 (1992), pp. 199–200.

7. Harold Bloom, *Shakespeare: The Invention of the Human* (New York: Riverhead Books, 1998), p. 33.

8. Diana E. Henderson, 'A Shrew for the Times', in *Shakespeare: The Movie, Popularizing the Plays on Film, TV, and Video*, edited by Lynda E. Boose and Richard Burt (London: Routledge, 1997), p. 161.

9. Frances E. Dolan, *The Taming of the Shrew: Texts and Contexts* (Boston: Bedford Books of St. Martin's Press, 1996), p. 254.

10. The evidence for the relative popularity of the two plays is not clear, however, since early records do not make a clear distinction between the two titles. For instance, Henslowe's reference to a June 1594 performance of 'the tamynge of A Shrowe' that netted only nine shillings may be further evidence of *The Taming of the Shrew*'s early lack of success if, as H. J. Oliver argued, the play in question was *The Taming of the Shrew* (Oxford edition, p. 32).

11. Tori Haring-Smith, *From Farce to Metadrama: A Stage History of The Taming of the Shrew, 1594–1983* (Westport, Conn. and London: Greenwood, 1985), p. 15.

12. *Catharine and Petruchio* (London: J. and R. Tonson, and S. Draper, 1756).

13. Janice A. Radway, *Reading the Romance: Women, Patriarchy, and Popular Literature* (Chapel Hill: University of North Carolina Press, 1984), p. 123.

14. These statistics come from a talk entitled 'The Substance of Romance', presented by Isabel Swift, the editorial head of Harlequin Enterprises, at the University of Pennsylvania in October 2002.

15. Sir Arthur Quiller-Couch, Introduction to *The Taming of the Shrew* (Cambridge: Cambridge University Press, 1928), p. xxv.

16. This phrase comes from Kathleen McLuskie's important and influential article, 'The Patriarchal Bard: Feminist Criticism and Shakespeare: *King Lear* and *Measure for Measure*', in *Political Shakespeare: Essays in Cultural Materialism*, edited by Jonathan Dollimore and Alan Sinfield, second edition (Ithaca: Cornell University Press, 1994).

17. In 'Scolding Brides and Bridling Scolds: Taming the Woman's Unruly Member', *Shakespeare Quarterly*, 42 (1991), Boose argues that historicizing the play requires attention to 'the realities that defined the lives of...the real village Kates who underwrite Shakespeare's character' (p. 181). Dolan's edition of the play—*The Taming of the Shrew: Texts and Contexts* (Bedford, 1996)—situates it in the context of an impressive array of Renaissance texts about marriage.

18. Although, as Leah Marcus points out, the locations in the Quarto are more generalized, allowing for the audience to imagine them in London rather than Windsor, both scripts seem clearly designed to evoke a familiar setting for their audiences. See 'Levelling Shakespeare: Local Customs and Local Texts', *Shakespeare Quarterly*, 42 (1991), pp. 173–5.

19. Letter CXXII in *Sociable Letters* (London: William Wilson, 1664).

20. Rosa Leo Grindon, *In Praise of Shakespeare's Merry Wives of Windsor: An Essay in Exposition and Appreciation* (Manchester: Sherratt and Hughes, 1902).

21. The index in Philip Kolin's *Shakespeare and Feminist Criticism: An Annotated Bibliography and Commentary* (New York and London: Garland, 1991), which covers the years 1975–88 has fifty-one entries for *The Taming of the Shrew* but only twenty-three for *The Merry Wives of Windsor*. In the last few years, however, there have been a number of excellent studies: Rosemary Kegl, ' "The adoption of abominable terms": Middle Classes, Merry Wives, and the Insults that Shape Windsor', in *The Rhetoric of*

Concealment: Figuring Gender and Class in Renaissance Literature (Ithaca: Cornell University Press, 1994), pp. 77–125; Richard Helgerson, 'The Buck Basket, the Witch, and the Queen of Fairies: The Women's World of Shakespeare's Windsor', in *Adulterous Alliances: Home, State, and History in Early Modern European Drama and Painting* (Chicago: University of Chicago Press, 2000), pp. 57–76; Wendy Wall, 'Why Does Puck Sweep? Shakespearean Fairies and the Politics of Cleaning', in *Staging Domesticity: Household Work and English Identity in Early Modern Drama* (Cambridge: Cambridge University Press, 2002), pp. 94–126, and '*The Merry Wives of Windsor*: Unhusbanding Desires in Windsor', in *A Companion to Shakespeare's Works: Volume III, The Comedies*, edited by Richard Dutton and Jean E. Howard (Oxford: Blackwell, 2003), pp. 376–92; Natasha Korda, 'Judicious Oeillades: Supervising Marital Property in *The Merry Wives of Windsor*', in *Shakespeare's Domestic Economies: Gender and Property in Early Modern England* (Philadelphia: University of Pennsylvania Press, 2002), pp. 76–110; and Lena Cowen Orlin, 'Shakespearean Comedy and Material Life', in Dutton and Howard, pp. 159–81.

22. Jeanne Addison Roberts, *Shakespeare's English Comedy: The Merry Wives of Windsor in Context* (Lincoln, Nebraska: University of Nebraska Press, 1979), pp. xi–xii, 65–6.

23. Charles Beecher Hogan, *Shakespeare in the Theatre* (Oxford: Clarendon Press, 1952), p. 460.

24. Bertrand H. Bronson (ed.), *Selections from Johnson on Shakespeare* (New Haven: Yale University Press, 1986), p. 129.

25. Andrew Lang, writing in *Harper's New Monthly Magazine*, LXXX (December 1889), p. 18.

26. Quoted by Walter Cohen in his introduction to the play in *The Norton Shakespeare*, edited by Stephen Greenblatt *et al.* (New York: W. W. Norton, 1997), p. 1225.

27. Felix Schelling, *Elizabethan Drama 1588–1642* (Boston: Houghton Mifflin, 1908), Vol. I, p. 324.

28. Frederick Wedmore, *The Academy*, 26 December 1874.

29. Arthur F. Kinney, 'Textual Signs in *The Merry Wives of Windsor*', *The Yearbook of Shakespeare Studies*, 3 (1993), p. 209.

30. William Hazlitt, *Characters of Shakespeare's Plays* (London: Oxford University Press, 1955), pp. 257–8.

31. Edward Dowden, *Shakspere: A Critical Study of His Mind and Art* (New York: Harper and Brothers, 1905), p. 329.

32. Hartley Coleridge, quoted in Dowden, p. 330. Bloom, p. 317. A. C. Bradley, 'The Rejection of Falstaff', *The Fortnightly Review*, LXXVII (May 1902), p. 849.

33. This reversal is of a piece with what seems to be the governing principle of Falstaff's characterization in *The Merry Wives*; for if the play was indeed designed as a showcase for Falstaff, it seems to have been conceived in a spirit of contradiction, as the very forces that provided the basis of Falstaff's power in the history plays are now mobilized against him. There he invoked material, physical life as the ultimate reality and *summum bonum*. Honour, he declared, was worthless, because it was a mere 'word', that could not 'set to a leg . . . or an arm. Or take away the grief of a wound' (*I Henry IV*: 5.1.127–39). In Windsor, he is confronted with the material world he opposed to the pieties of history and made to suffer a series of punishments that are all physical.

34. Valerie Traub, *Desire and Anxiety: Circulations of Sexuality in Shakespearean Drama* (London: Routledge, 1992), pp. 50–70; Phyllis Rackin, 'Historical Difference/Sexual Difference', in *Privileging Gender in Early Modern Britain*, edited by J. Brink (Kirksville, Mo.: Sixteenth Century Journal Publishers, 1992), pp. 37–63.

CHAPTER 4

1. Letter CXXII in *Sociable Letters* (London: William Wilson, 1664).
2. *Toward a Recognition of Androgyny* (New York: Alfred A. Knopf, 1973), pp. 30–4.
3. See Marianne Novy (ed.), *Women's Re-Visions of Shakespeare* (Urbana and Chicago: University of Illinois Press, 1990); and Ann Thompson and Sasha Roberts (eds.), *Women Reading Shakespeare 1660–1900: An Anthology of Criticism* (Manchester: Manchester University Press, 1997).
4. Quoted by Georgianna Ziegler, in *Shakespeare's Unruly Women* (Washington: Folger Shakespeare Library, 1997), p. 17.
5. Of course, advocates for women are not the only writers who have assumed that Shakespeare's female characters were convincing portraits of actual women. Even those scholars who have taken a generally pessimistic view of women's place in Shakespeare's world often cite the plays for evidence to support their arguments. A striking example, noted in Chapter I, is Anthony Fletcher's *Gender, Sex and Subordination in England 1500–1800*, which contains no less than fifty-four references to Shakespeare's plays.
6. *Coryate's Crudities* (1611), p. 247, quoted in Gerald Eades Bentley, *The Profession of Player in Shakespeare's Time* (Princeton: Princeton University Press, 1984), p. 114.
7. *Roscius Anglicanus* (London, 1708), p. C2, quoted in Bentley (1984), p. 115.

8. *Shakespeare and the Nature of Women* (London: Macmillan, 1975), p. 271.

9. 'Disrupting Sexual Difference: Meaning and Gender in the Comedies', in *Alternative Shakespeares*, edited by John Drakakis (London and New York: Methuen, 1985), p. 183.

10. 'Fiction and Friction', in *Shakespearean Negotiations: The Circulation of Social Energy in Renaissance England* (Berkeley and Los Angeles: University of California Press, 1988), p. 93.

11. *Still Harping on Daughters: Women and Drama in the Age of Shakespeare* (Sussex: Harvester Press, 1983), pp. 29, 31.

12. Ann Thompson, 'Women/"women" and the stage', in *Women and Literature in Britain 1500–1700*, edited by Helen Wilcox (Cambridge: Cambridge University Press, 1996); Elizabeth Howe, *The First English Actresses: Women and Drama 1660–1700* (Cambridge: Cambridge University Press, 1992), pp. 26–37.

13. Contemporary documents refer to the titles of numerous plays whose texts are now entirely lost: the papers of the theatre manager Philip Henslowe, for instance, give the names of 280 plays, only forty of which have survived. In addition, scholars have estimated that there were probably about 500 plays for which even the titles have been lost (James P. Saeger and Christopher Fassler, 'The London Professional Theater, 1576–1642: A Catalogue and Analysis of the Extant Printed Plays', *Research Opportunities in Renaissance Drama*, 34 (1995), p. 63).

14. The definitive analysis of the antitheatrical arguments can be found in Jean E. Howard, *The Stage and Social Struggle in Early Modern England* (London and New York: Routledge, 1994).

15. *Playes Confuted in Five Actions* (1582), in E. K. Chambers, *The Elizabethan Stage* (Oxford: Clarendon Press, 1923), Vol. IV, p. 217.

16. On the significance of the name Proteus, see Jonas Barish, *The Antitheatrical Prejudice* (Berkeley: University of California Press, 1975), pp. 99–107.

17. 'Shakespeare and Cultural Difference', in *Alternative Shakespeares*, Vol. II, edited by Terence Hawkes (London and New York: Routledge, 1996), p. 175.

18. From an interview entitled 'Mr. Shaw on Heroes', signed A.D., *Liverpool Post*, 19 October 1927.

19. William Rankins, *A Mirror of Monsters* (1587), cited by Jyotsna Singh, 'Renaissance Anti-theatricality, Anti-feminism, and Shakespeare's "Antony and Cleopatra" ', *Renaissance Drama*, 20 (1989), p. 105.

20. Mary Hamer, *Signs of Cleopatra: History, Politics, Representation* (London: Routledge, 1993), p. 29.

21. Carol Cook, 'The Fatal Cleopatra', in *Shakespearean Tragedy and Gender*, edited by Shirley Nelson Garner and Madelon Spengnether (Bloomington: Indiana University Press, 1996), p. 243.

22. 'Preface' (1765) in *Selections from Johnson on Shakespeare*, edited by Bertrand H. Bronson and Jean M. O'Meara (New Haven: Yale University Press, 1986), p. 22.

23. Letter CXXII in *Sociable Letters* (London: William Wilson, 1664). See Chapter 3 for Cavendish's exact words.

24. Linda T. Fitz (Woodbridge), 'Egyptian Queens and Male Reviewers', in *Antony and Cleopatra: Contemporary Critical Essays*, edited by John Drakakis (London: Macmillan, 1994), p. 184.

25. Irene Dash, *Wooing, Wedding, and Power: Women in Shakespeare's Plays* (New York: Columbia University Press, 1981), p. 246.

26. *Shakespeare without Women: Representing Gender and Race on the Renaissance Stage* (London and New York: Routledge, 2000), pp. 13–14.

CHAPTER 5

1. Nancy J. Vickers, 'Diana Described: Scattered Woman and Scattered Rhyme', in *Writing and Sexual Difference*, edited by Elizabeth Abel (Chicago: University of Chicago Press, 1982), p. 96.

2. Morris Bishop, *Petrarch and His World* (Bloomington: Indiana University Press, 1963), p. 329.

3. Elizabeth Cropper, 'On Beautiful Women, Parmigianino, *Petrarchismo*, and the Vernacular Style', *Art Bulletin*, 58 (1976), p. 376, quoted by Vickers, p. 107.

4. *A Casebook on Shakespeare's Sonnets*, edited by Gerald Willen and Victor B. Reed (New York: Thomas Y. Crowell, 1964), p. 132 n. A significant exception to the chorus of editorial denial is G. Blakemore Evans's 1996 New Cambridge edition.

5. These examples come from the *Oxford English Dictionary*. The 1563 example is 'Thai knaw thair stink to na man almaist . . . to be plesand, gif it stewit and reikit out naikit and plane'. Compare the 2002 Oxford edition of the sonnets, in which Colin Burrow notes that 'The sense "to stink" is not recorded before the eighteenth century'.

6. Quoted by Bonnie S. Anderson and Judith P. Zinsser, *A History of Their Own: Women in Europe from Prehistory to the Present* (New York: Harper and Row, 1988), Vol. I, p. 83.

7. Rosalie Osmond, *Mutual Accusation: Seventeenth-Century Body and Soul Dialogues in Their Literary and Theological Context* (Toronto: University of Toronto Press, 1990).

8. Gerrard Winstanley, *The New Law of Righteousness*, in *The Works of Gerrard Winstanley*, edited by George H. Sabine (Ithaca: Cornell University Press, 1941), p. 157. See also Allison P. Coudert, 'The Myth of the Improved Status of Protestant Women: The Case of the Witchcraze', in *The Politics of Gender in Early Modern Europe*, edited by Jean R. Brink, Allison P. Coudert, and Maryanne C. Horowitz, *Sixteenth Century Essays and Studies*, XII (1989), p. 81.

9. Margreta de Grazia, 'The Scandal of Shakespeare's Sonnets', *Shakespeare Survey*, 46 (1994), pp. 35–49.

10. 'Anti-hermeneutics: The Case of Shakespeare's Sonnet 129', in *Poetic Traditions of the English Renaissance*, edited by Maynard Mack and George deForest Lord (New Haven: Yale University Press, 1982), p. 148. Cf. Michel Foucault's argument in *The Use of Pleasure: Volume 2 of the History of Sexuality*, trans. Robert Hurley (New York: Vintage Books, 1990), pp. 82–6 that for the Greeks the 'dividing line between a virile man and an effeminate man did not coincide with our opposition between hetero- and homosexuality' but instead distinguished a man who yielded to his appetites from one who exercised control over them. Rebecca W. Bushnell demonstrates the persistence of this idea in Renaissance representations of tyrants in *Tragedies of Tyrants: Political Thought and Theater in the English Renaissance* (Ithaca: Cornell University Press, 1990).

11. Alan Sinfield, *The Wilde Century: Effeminacy, Oscar Wilde and the Queer Moment* (London: Cassell, 1994).

12. *Shakespere's Sonnets*, edited by Stephen Booth (New Haven and London: Yale University Press, 1977), p. 452.

13. *A Window to Criticism: Shakespeare's Sonnets and Modern Poetics* (Princeton: Princeton University Press, 1964), pp. 78–9.

14. *Republic*, Book VI, 508, in *The Dialogues of Plato*, trans. B. Jowett, fourth edition (Oxford: Clarendon Press, 1953), Vol. II, p. 370.

CHAPTER 6

1. Samuel Burdett Hemingway (ed.), the Variorum edition of Shakespeare's *Henry the Fourth, Part I* (Philadelphia and London: J. B. Lippincott, 1936), p. 174 n.

2. Katherine Eggert, 'Age Cannot Wither Him: Warren Beatty's Bugsy as Hollywood's Cleopatra', in *Shakespeare the Movie: Popularizing the Plays on Film, TV, and Video*, edited by Lynda E. Boose and Richard Burt (London and New York: Routledge, 1997), pp. 198–214.

3. Mary Hamer, *Signs of Cleopatra: History, Politics, Representation* (London: Routledge, 1993), pp. 34–44.

4. The only exception was an unsuccessful revival staged by David Garrick in 1759.
5. *All for Love*, edited by N. J. Andrew (London: Ernest Benn Ltd., New Mermaids, 1975), p. 11.
6. Georgianna Ziegler, with Frances E. Dolan and Jeanne Addison Roberts, *Shakespeare's Unruly Women* (Washington: The Folger Shakespeare Library, 1997), p. 75.
7. 'General Macbeth', originally published in *Harper's Magazine* (June 1962), reprinted in the Signet Classic Edition of *Macbeth*, edited by Sylvan Barnet (New York: New American Library, 1963), p. 234.
8. Natalie Angier, 'Goddesses, Harlots and Other Male Fantasies', review of Marilyn Yalom, *A History of the Breast* (New York: Alfred A. Knopf, 1997), in *The New York Times Book Review*, 23 February, 1997, p. 4. See also Yalom, pp. 87–9.
9. Caroline Walker Bynum, *Holy Feast and Holy Fast: The Religious Significance of Food to Medieval Women* (Berkeley: University of California Press, 1987), pp. 270–1. See also Londa Schiebinger, 'Why Mammals are Called Mammals', *American Historical Review* (April 1993), p. 398.
10. Bradbrook, 'The Sources of Macbeth', *ShS*, 4 (1951), pp. 35–48. Raphael Holinshed, *Chronicles of England, Scotland and Ireland*, second edition 1587 (reprinted London: J. Johnson *et al.*, 1808), Vol. 5, pp. 22–7. 'Holinshed's' is shorthand: the *Chronicles* included the work of many writers—predecessors whose work had been incorporated, successors who augmented the narrative after Holinshed's death, and collaborators at the time of its original production. The 'Description of Scotland', for instance, was translated by William Harrison from a Scots translation by John Bellenden of Hector Boece's (or Boethius's) early sixteenth-century Latin text *Historia Scotorum*.
11. Nina Auerbach, *Ellen Terry: Player in Her Time* (New York: Norton, 1987), p. 352.
12. Holinshed, Vol. 5, pp. 23–4 (my italics).
13. Thomas Laqueur, *Making Sex: Body and Gender from the Greeks to Freud* (Cambridge, Mass.: Harvard University Press, 1990), p. 149.
14. Valerie Fildes, *Breasts, Bottles and Babies: A History of Infant Feeding* (Edinburgh: Edinburgh University Press, 1986), p. 100.
15. Photographs of these inscriptions can be found in Fildes, pp. 100, 101.
16. Both quotations come from a list of similar statements in Fildes, p. 104, which also includes William Gouge's observation in his 1622 treatise *Of Domestical Duties*, 'Husbands for the most part are the cause that their wives nurse not their owne children' and James Nelson's claim in his 1753 *Essay on the Government of Children* that 'many a tender mother, has her

heart yearning to suckle her child, and is prevented by the misplac'd authority of a husband'.

17. Craig Thompson (ed. and trans.), Desiderius Erasmus, 'The New Mother (*Puerpera*)', in *The Colloquies of Erasmus* (Chicago: University of Chicago Press, 1965), p. 267.

18. Some women still used wetnurses in England, however, and the practice remained customary on the Continent. In *The Family, Sex and Marriage in England 1500–1800* (New York: Harper and Row, 1977), p. 430, Lawrence Stone quotes a German visitor who visited England in 1784 and 'remarked with surprise' that 'even women of quality nurse their children'.

19. Susan Cahn, *Industry of Devotion: The Transformation of Women's Work in England, 1500–1660* (New York: Columbia University Press, 1987), pp. 104–5.

20. Thomas Tusser, *The Points of Housewifery* (1580), in Joan Larsen Klein (ed.) *Daughters' Wives and Widows: Writings by Men about Women and Marriage in England, 1500–1640* (Urbana: University of Illinois Press, 1992), p. 228.

21. Stone, p. 428.

22. *The Female Spectator: English Women Writers before 1800*, Mary R. Mahl and Helene Koon (eds.) (Old Westbury, NY: Feminist Press, 1977), pp. 89–98.

23. *Certaine Plaine, briefe, and Comfortable Notes upon every Chapter of Genesis* (London, 1592), quoted in Cahn, p. 105.

24. Gail Kern Paster, *The Body Embarrassed: Drama and the Disciplines of Shame in Early Modern England* (Ithaca: Cornell University Press, 1992), p. 201.

25. Stone, pp. 63–6. Dorothy McLaren, 'Marital fertility and lactation 1570–1720', in Mary Prior (ed.), *Women in English Society 1500–1800* (London and New York: Methuen, 1985), p. 43.

26. Cambridge: The Minority Press, 1933.

27. *Shakespeare and his Plays from a Woman's Point of View* (reprinted Manchester : Policy-Holder Journal Co. Ltd., 1930), pp. 8–9.

28. Davenant's version held the stage from the 1660s until 1774. See Philip Bordinat and Sophia B. Blaydes, *Sir William Davenant* (Boston: G. K. Hall, 1981), p. 141.

Index

Italic numbers denote references to illustrations

168   *Index*

Lightning Source UK Ltd.
Milton Keynes UK
13 January 2010

148507UK00001BA/7/P